Shifting into
Higher Gear

Shifting into Higher Gear

**AN OWNER'S MANUAL
FOR UNITING YOUR
CALLING AND CAREER**

Tom Siciliano
Jeff Caliguire

JOSSEY-BASS
A Wiley Imprint
www.josseybass.com

Published by Jossey-Bass
A Wiley Imprint
989 Market Street, San Francisco, CA 94103-1741 www.josseybass.com

Jossey-Bass books and products are available through most bookstores. To contact Jossey-Bass directly call our Customer Care Department within the U.S. at 800-956-7739, outside the U.S. at 317-572-3993 or fax 317-572-4002.

Jossey-Bass also publishes its books in a variety of electronic formats. Some content that appears in print may not be available in electronic books.

Library of Congress Cataloging-in-Publication Data

Siciliano, Tom
    Shifting into higher gear : an owner's manual for uniting your calling and career / Tom Siciliano, Jeff Caliguire.— 1st ed.
        p. cm.
    Includes bibliographical references.
    ISBN-13 978-0-7879-7372-8
    ISBN-10 0-7879-7372-6 (alk. paper)
    1. Vocational guidance—Handbooks, manuals, etc. 2. Career development—Handbooks, manuals, etc. 3. Job hunting—Handbooks, manuals, etc. I. Caliguire, Jeff. II. Title.
HF5381.S445 2005
650.14—dc22

2004030327

FIRST EDITION
PB Printing 10 9 8 7 6 5 4 3 2 1

Contents

God created a great woman in Suzi, who has the grace of an angel, the strength of a warrior, and the love of a saint. You are my rock and my compass. Thanks for bringing color and your amazing love into my life.

—T. S.

To Mindy—my sweetheart and partner in the adventure of living life to the fullest. You're a gift to me, to our J-Team, and to many others.

—J. C.

Acknowledgments

THIS BOOK has been an ongoing project for more than two years. During that time we received encouragement and support from many great people. First, we'd like to thank the folks at Jossey-Bass, especially our editors, Julianna Gustafson and Chandrika Madhavanwho helped us through this project, as well as Liah Rose at Interactive Composition who helped us pull it all together and finish the project. In addition, our agent and great friend, Mark Gilroy, believed in us and encouraged us when we needed it most.

We thank all those who had to listen to us at coffee shops, bookstores, hotels, and other crazy places as we argued, discussed, and laughed out loud. Thanks to our wives, Suzi and Mindy, who gave up nights, weekends, and dreams of their own as we worked on this project.

I (Jeff) thank my children—Jeffery, Jonathan, and Josh—who played quietly so that we could work. Josh, thanks for making us laugh during those late nights. I (Tom) thank my children, Luke and Leila, who teach me every day how to be a better person and dad. You have taught me how to love. You both amaze me with your love, compassion, and honesty. Keep teaching me, I have much to learn.

We thank our extended family. I (Tom) thank my parents, Tony and Pat Siciliano, for their stories and support, for providing a great foundation and being great role models. I (Jeff) thank my parents, Bob and Gloria Caliguire, who buy more of my books than they should. Thanks to our brothers and sisters: Todd and Mark, who knew me (Jeff) as their pain-in-the-neck little brother; and Don, Mike, and Terri, who knew me (Tom) as their pain-in-the-neck older brother.

We thank people who have inspired us by their writing and teaching: Ken Blanchard, Bill Hybels, Mark Jankowski, Peter Leffkowitz, Ralph Mattson, Pam Rotter, and Ron Shapiro.

Thanks go to George Parthemore and Dick McDowell, who were the first ones who truly believed in me (Tom) and taught me through their leadership how to be a great leader and help others grow.

Thanks to our band of real brothers and sisters who keep us sane and encourage us to keep writing: Matt McConaughy, my (Tom's) trusted friend and confidant, for his support, friendship, and passion and for challenging me to be my best; Pat Lambert, my friend of thirty years; John Gillie; Dan Mathews; and all my prayer warriors. I (Jeff) thank my team: Frank, Chris, Vance, Gregg, and Bruce, as well as my Friday night group, the MJM Group at Smith Barney, and all those on my prayer-warrior team.

Thanks to the entire LifeWork team at Willow Creek, especially Mike Patterson and Ruth Groth, who taught me (Tom) more than I ever taught them. It's here that the real foundation for this book started.

I (Tom) thank Jeff Caliguire, who started out as just the ghostwriter for this book and became first my friend and then a great partner and contributor during this long project. I also thank recording artist Dan Fogelberg, who has helped me to believe that a kid from Illinois can stand up and be heard and do what he believes.

We are sure we are missing many others who have served, taught, and encouraged us. We say a sincere thanks for all your support even when we didn't deserve it. We give thanks to you all.

Tom Siciliano and Jeff Caliguire

Introduction

When man loses the sacred significance of work and of himself as worker, he soon loses the sacred meaning of time and of life.

—Carl F. H. Henry, *Philosopher*

THOUGH HE WASN'T MISERABLE, Matt wasn't satisfied either. He wondered if it was time for a change. Over a couple of iced teas at a coffee shop, he shared with us. "I'd really like to do something I enjoy this time. Not just another job. Something significant. Something I'm good at. But honestly, I can't afford to risk getting a job I'll want to leave in a couple of years. I can't afford to experiment. I still need to make a living."

Despite all the progress in communications and technology, many of us, like Matt, still wonder what we're supposed to do with our work lives. We wonder if there's a way to find the right job besides pure chance, hit-and-miss networking, or scanning endless job postings. Of course, we don't want to settle for any job we can get. But still we may wonder, *Is there something out there we're supposed to be doing?* Is there something we might even enjoy doing? In a world with endless options, which path do we follow? Is there a technology that would help us navigate the maze of professional life?

After meeting with person after person with similar nagging questions, we (Tom and Jeff) wondered if we might develop a better way. We had experienced this stumbling in the dark ourselves. If the philosophies of calling, life work, vocation, or giftedness were for real, why didn't more people seem to experience their work on some level as a true calling?

Soon after we met, we began talking about our common beliefs about calling and career. We quickly realized that we held similar convictions and a common desire to serve people who were trapped, or at least unfulfilled, in this area of life. We began working on a process that could help people have greater energy to approach their work. Both of us felt that many more people could head confidently in the right direction if they knew what they were made to do, not just what they could do. And if they had help in this area, they could live in a career, not just work a job.

We both come at this issue from the perspective of trying to help people.

In my (Jeff) work as a financial adviser with individuals and companies, I am passionate about helping them operate according to their unique strengths. My own experience of career stress and my journey of intense self-reflection has caused me to become interested in helping others settle for nothing less than what they're great at. I also guide personal and group retreats and coach those seeking to unlock the potential in their career, leadership, and life. I help them get to the next level of their potential or to define and engage their dream.

I (Tom) teach those who seek jobs and work with companies looking for great employees who fit their needs. My career calling is to inspire and encourage people to be their best and find value in their life work. From starting my career as a forklift driver to finding myself responsible for hundreds of people and millions of dollars as a vice president of sales, I've been drawn to help people seeking the right career. My passion is to help them find the jobs that fit their strengths. Though I received much of my own education and experience from costly mistakes, I now seek to share the shortcuts I've learned and to pass on the formula for finding a career fit I missed out on.

The fact that you're reading this may mean that you want to move to the next level in your career or that you want to find a job. But rather than finding just another job, you are interested in **finding the job that fits your calling.** We won't promise you a job, but we can promise that reading this book and doing the exercises will help you focus your quest and give you tools for a lifetime.

We invite you on a journey that will likely stretch you. It involves practices like reflection, introspection, and the creation of a written strategy to focus your search. It may provide an opportunity for you to step back and examine questions floating around inside you. Don't we all at times look up at the stars and wonder, *Can I find and fulfill the central purpose of my life? If so, how?*

You will evaluate the clues of your own design, be able to articulate what you do best, then attain the job you've been gifted to do. If all goes well, you will unlock career potential that's been dormant or is just now ready for full expression. Our goal is to encourage and inspire you to be you. You really can do what you were created to do. You can live out your calling. You have the ability to attain a job you love. Why shoot for anything less? As Michelangelo said, "The greater danger for most of us is not that our aim is too high and we miss it, but that it is too low and we reach it."[1]

We've created a formula to help you find that position. Our intention is to help you know why and how to shift your life into higher gear in the area of career and calling. Driving a Porsche in first or second gear on the open highway would be a waste of time. Similarly, your higher gear awaits you to engage, explore, and experience.

This journey of making your calling your career may involve going against traffic and moving into unexplored territory. You may need to ignore voices from your childhood and even the voices of your peers or the career counselors in your past. This journey may mean gaining the courage to go after the job you've only dreamed of. If you do so, you will succeed in living the life you were made for. You will express your gifts, your skills, your values—maybe for the rest of your life!

If you're wanting to make that shift, the following pages will help you succeed.

Tom Siciliano and Jeff Caliguire

Shifting into
Higher Gear

Discovering Your Calling

CHAPTER 1

The Four Laws of Calling

JUST AS physical laws govern the universe and criminal laws protect us as citizens, there are laws that relate to work, career, and calling. By *calling*, we're talking about the intentionality of your design and purpose. It's being in alignment with what you've been created to do and your ability to do something with excellence and passion. It's accepting who you are and responding to the voice that says, "This is who you are. This is what you were made to do. Now do it."

As we begin this journey with you, we encourage you to shift into higher gear and trust yourself as you step out into faith.

Try as we might, none of us escapes the laws of calling—at least not for long. When we obey them, these laws liberate and protect us. When we break them, we experience the consequences.

> *Chapter Take-Aways*
>
> - Don't compare yourself with others in areas of calling.
> - Focus your career by studying clues from your past.
> - Discover the reasons to find and follow your calling.

But what about those of us who never knew about the laws of calling (that is, almost all of us)? We weren't schooled to know how to find them nor even to know that such laws existed. Just as with the laws of society or science, ignorance of a law does not negate the law.

Many of us discover the laws of calling as we do other laws: by breaking them, by finding that something doesn't work or achieve the desired results. As kids, our ignorance of the laws of gravity didn't stop us from climbing to the window ledge, flapping our "wings," and leaping. But we did experience gravity the old-fashioned way—with a thud. We couldn't escape the grasp of other laws either. When we stuck a fork in those three little holes in the wall as children, we experienced the power of positive and negative currents. When we pushed the pedal to the metal as young adults, we sometimes experienced the sound of sirens, the flashing lights in the rearview mirror, and the officer's walk to our car.

Try as you might to escape or disregard their existence or their grasp, you live in a world of laws. So when it comes to finding and engaging your calling or career, you will need to understand, accept, and live in harmony with these laws.

Here's Reality

People who promote finding a good job like to say that you can do anything you set your mind to. We're here to tell you otherwise. **You can't do anything you want.** That's right: you can't do absolutely *anything* you want. There are some things you were never meant to do. No matter how hard you work or how much a job pays, if it's not your thing, don't waste your time.

The foundation for these laws is that your success may look nothing like anyone else's. Comparing yourself to others doesn't work. You've sensed this truth, even if living it out has been almost impossible. You're different. You have unique abilities and a unique set of life experiences, training, and family history. So success is not something you attain. Instead it's a full and free expression of your unique abilities. It's all about doing what you are and not about becoming something because of what you do. As you unlock the gates to your inner springs, living waters will flow in you and through your work—not in drive, compulsion, and striving but in the same way a river flows downstream—because it just can't help itself!

The starting place to find your career and calling isn't trying to gain something you don't have. Instead it's about becoming confident and secure in what you *do* have. It's becoming excited about the real you.

So take a deep breath. Relax. It's OK. You don't have to be good at everything. In fact, you don't have to be good at most things. You simply need to grow in confidence and in courage to boldly express what you do have. And this book is here to equip you to do just that.

So if you don't live out your calling, who will? If you don't use your gifts, who will? And though the impact of this may not be immediately obvious, what happens in a society where the majority of people neither realize they have a calling nor live it out? What potential remains untapped? What creativity, design, inventions, or production never finds its way into the world?

Ultimately, calling involves

- What you're good at
- What you've gained experience in
- What you dream about
- Where your passion lies
- Where you have confidence to perform

And you don't miss out when you focus on your call and let others follow theirs. In fact, as you express yourself through your calling, as you step up and accept that baton, you actually discover more energy than you ever knew you possessed! You give out only what you've been given and find what you've been given to be plentiful and quickly replenished. Besides the fact that you live in obedience to a higher law, you also discover the benefits of peace, a sense of purpose, and the potential to achieve excellence rather than mediocrity.

When you obey the law of calling and live in line with it, you find blessing and freedom. When you go against it, you suffer the consequences. As Cecil B. De Mille, the famous director of the movie *The Ten Commandments*, said, "You either break the law, or you are broken by it."[1]

At this point you may just want to skip to the how-to-find-a-job section. We don't blame you. For many of us, this kind of reflective process doesn't come easy. It may even feel like fluff, something way too abstract or spiritual. But stick with this. If this is your only chance to do the hard work of finding your calling, it may be the work that changes your life.

Law One: You Can Do Something Really Well

At times you may have compared yourself to another and thought, *I can't do anything that well!* Stop listening to what people say. You can do something really well—your thing! Don't let other people determine what that is. Maybe as a kid you struggled with math, spelling, history, and grammar but excelled at shop and penmanship. We all function differently. Personality styles and abilities differ. Anyone can put on a basketball jersey with the number twenty-three on the back, but that doesn't make them Michael Jordan!

I (Tom) always tell people to just get in trouble. You get in trouble when you speak the truth without worry or concern about pleasing everyone or looking good. Troublemakers push forward with what they believe is right, authentic, and meaningful. Quit worrying about what could happen and focus on your goals. A few months ago, I told a management candidate in his forties, "Stop worrying about what others think. Don't lie, steal, or cheat. Be a trout and swim upstream. Don't let anyone tell you, 'You can't do that.'"

Though some laws restrict us, the laws of calling liberate us. They set us free to experience our lives, authenticity, and fullness. When he was an old man, Rabbi Zusya, a Hasidic Jewish teacher, said, "In the coming world, they will not ask me: 'Why were you not Moses?' They will ask me: 'Why were you not Zusya?'"[2] Though the word *calling* seems slightly mystical, ultimately the concept is about living our lives, playing the music inside of us, and not our mother's, father's, or teacher's.

Law Two: You Are Unique

Every cell of your body holds the unique DNA code that makes you special. There never has and never will be another you. God created you purposefully and with intention.

Your physical traits, your personality, as well as your gifts, skills, and natural abilities equip you to act in a way that fits you. Only you can do the work you do in the way you do it. Once you add your portfolio of experiences, training, and interests to the mix, you find there are certain things you're uniquely equipped to do. There are ideas and designs that flow from your mind and tasks you do best.

Here's the good news:

- You don't need to measure up to anyone else.

- There's no mold for you to fit in order to be a success.

- There are tasks that you are uniquely equipped to do.

- There will never be another you.

Law Three: Your Past Holds Clues to Your Future

The past doesn't determine your future, but it contains clues that can help you see what you've been created to do. Have you ever noticed that you tend to remember certain moments more vividly than others? You go back to them as if they're bookmarked. They remain as a picture or a defining moment.

Here are some examples of defining moments from people we met with:

> I taught my next-door neighbor how to ride her bike. I can still remember shouting with excitement when she took off on her own!

> I recruited the kids on my block to open a lemonade stand. We all made a lot of money for a bunch of little kids!

> I was asked to play the lead role in the junior high school play. It was the greatest honor I had ever had!

> I made the dean's list in college three years in a row. I loved to study and learn new things.

> I was promoted to supervisor within a year of joining the company in the lowest ranks. I just kept getting promoted until I was asked to be CEO.

How do you feel when you accomplish something you feel uniquely suited for? You feel great, don't you? As you look back at your accomplishments, you feel energized, alive, fulfilled. Might those past accomplishments be significant clues to help you build future accomplishments?

People-design experts Ralph Mattson and Arthur Miller write, "People do things. The way a person does them, and what he or she intends to accomplish, is not caused by chance. You will find embedded in his or her actions a unique, consistent pattern. In other words, we all have individual likes and dislikes."[3] In other words, what you do and don't do says a lot about you; and your actions often form patterns that express your purest motivations.

Worksheet 1.1 is an exercise that will help you figure out your own purest motivations by exploring the past. So get ready to dig in.

Motivated Memory Clues Worksheet

Exercise: Off the top of your head, list accomplishments in the different areas mentioned here. Don't overthink this. Just recall positive memories that you feel good about. Write down any past accomplishments that quickly come to mind: times that you set out to do something and got it done.

Childhood Until Junior High

1. _____
2. _____
3. _____

Teen Years (High School and College)

1. _____
2. _____
3. _____

In the Workplace

1. _____
2. _____
3. _____

Most Recent Accomplishments

1. _____
2. _____
3. _____

Now examine the clues.

Do you see any patterns? _____
_____
_____

What abilities stick out? _____
_____
_____

What seemed to get you going or inspire your actions? _____
_____
_____

Law Four: You Have Something the World Needs

Author Frederick Buechner asserts that your vocation is "the place where your deep gladness meets the world's deepest need."[4] The assumptions here are that (1) you have a passion and (2) some place in the world needs what you have. It's supply and demand.

It takes an incredible and diverse workforce to run our world. Not everyone can be a doctor, carpenter, or CEO. Some are philosophers, painters, executive recruiters, financial advisers, and writers. In the New Testament, Paul compares this working diversity to the functioning of a healthy body. He writes in the letter to Corinthians (12:14–15,19 NIV), "Now the body is not made up of one part, but of many. If the foot should say, 'Because I am a hand, I do not belong to the body,' it would not for that reason cease to be part of the body. If they were all one part where would the body be? As it is there are many parts, but one body."

What you were created to do matters to the rest of us just as the foot matters to the healthy body. When you do the job that fits your calling, the world becomes a better place. Like the music teacher in the movie *Mr. Holland's Opus,* you may ask yourself, "Has it been worth it?"[5] (or "Will it be worth it?"). Only you can answer that question, and the people you serve may never give you a standing ovation, a gold watch, or the salary you deserve. But things function when teachers teach and doctors diagnose and builders build.

How might you evaluate your present situation in light of the laws of calling?

- ❑ Excellent! A perfect fit!
- ❑ Good. I'm pretty much in the zone.
- ❑ Fair. Sometimes I'm there, sometimes not.
- ❑ Poor. I need to reevaluate what I'm doing and where I'm headed.
- ❑ Lousy. I need major changes.

If you checked one of the last three statements, we're going to help you make the laws of calling part of your life.

CHAPTER 2

Spiritual Clues

A WHITE FEATHER drifts silently through the blue sky, headed toward earth. It's blown this way and that above roadways and rooftops while life happens far below. The feather settles on the lap of an ordinary man wearing a white suit. Is it random? Fate? Or just the magic of a movie?

If you've seen the movie *Forrest Gump,* you may recall this scene. Soon after his beloved Jenny dies, Forrest reflects on his life's meaning. You may be able to picture him. Head tilted, brow furrowed, Forrest asks the simple yet penetrating question of life: "Are we created for some kind of purpose or are we just floating around accidental-like with the wind?"[1] Can you relate to this question? Do you sometimes feel like that feather? *Am I created for some kind of purpose, or am I "just floating around accidental-like with the wind?"*

> ## *Chapter Take-Aways*
>
> - Identify moments when God's purpose was revealed most clearly and you sensed your calling being fulfilled.
> - Discover your spiritual gifts through a checklist with definitions to help you use your gifts.
> - Identify your three top spiritual gifts.

In this chapter we invite you to carefully examine the spiritual clues that point to your career calling and might help you answer Forrest's question. Let's shift into spiritual gear.

You may or may not perceive a spiritual work happening all around you. Some people do. For example, they see it as more than coincidence that a parking space opened up right in front of the store they were heading to just before the storm hit. They see design in the roughest situations. A middle-aged woman says she saw God at work in her battle with cancer. Others go to the opposite extreme and live in fatalism: "Ah, bad stuff happens!" Yet when spiritually visioned people speak, they see purposeful intent behind vivid or unusual dreams, déjà vu ("I've been here before") moments, or even what might seem to most as ordinary life.

We believe that when it comes to investigating something as important as your life calling and work, spiritual clues are too valuable to ignore. This is not to say that you should invent what doesn't exist or that finding your calling won't take some work. Busyness and even temptation toward fear and self-centeredness will fight against you all the way. But here's the gold in this chapter: if you would just venture away from your routine, your to-do list, and your own background noise, your career search might lead you to a place more important than salaries, budgets, and benefits. And maybe, as Rick Warren has said in his book *The Purpose Driven Life,* you will come to see that "It's not all about you."[2] There's a bigger plan being worked out in all of this stuff, and your decision matters—not just for you but for a larger purpose.

This may feel a bit awkward at first, particularly if you've been running fast for some time. You may be saying, "Come on guys, let's get past the touchy-feely stuff and into the how-to-land-a-job stuff."

We say back: stop talking and start listening. You have ears—use them!

But we also realize that at this juncture, you may not be ready for the challenge of this chapter. And if so, we understand and invite you to skip over it. So if you continue, you are saying, "I am at least open to examining the spiritual clues to my calling, and I'm willing to explore those possibilities."

If that's the case, we would like to share with you four ways you might examine the spiritual clues in your life right now.

Listen to Your Life

You would think it would be natural for us to listen to our lives. For most of us, it's not. Our educational experiences tend to focus us on learning what's out *there.* We've all sat through lectures on ancient history, health, and biology. You may have attended seminars on improving your performance and managing your time. But where do you learn how to get guidance through what happens and what doesn't happen in your own life?

Even high schools and colleges would do the world a great service if they included at least some focused coursework on how to listen for clues to vocation, life mission, and overall good living in their curriculum. Imagine the potential that could be released in students if they took classes such as doing what you're great at or finding your life's work. This might be the kind of thing that could be taught through a local church, synagogue, or community center.

The first priority of listening to your life is to seek guidance in taking your next step toward growth. We believe that life is a journey of becoming the people we were created to be. This is the essence of spiritual growth. Spiritual growth isn't an invitation to step out of ordinary life to become religious, weird, or monkish. It's not about leaving the world or entering a certain vocation. Just the opposite: when you grow spiritually, you become fully and unapologetically *you*. You become freer, happier, and more whole. As the Danish theologian Søren Kierkegaard put it, "Now with God's help I shall become myself."[3]

To grow spiritually is to become truly healthy. When you use your gifts, you find yourself in harmony with the purpose and mission God has created for you to complete. The result is energy and a sense of peace. Another result is harmony in relationships because others experience you as free to be you—no longer competing or clawing for recognition.

One of the main reasons we're so passionate to share the message and process of this book is because we've both tried to create and control our own destinies. We ignored the voice of calling and instead sought to follow our own misguided counsel.

I (Tom) vividly recall driving one early morning to a sales appointment in rural Iowa. As I looked on the map, I noticed I was right near the town of Dyersville. That may not mean anything to a lot of people, but to me, it was like seeing a sign that said: Entering the Holy Land. Dyersville is where the baseball movie *Field of Dreams* was shot. I headed straight for that field. When I arrived, I found myself completely alone as the mist rose from the field. As I stood at the edge of that cornfield, I pictured scenes from the movie. But I also considered the deeper meaning of my presence there. *Tom, are you going to be like Roy, hearing voices from the past someday? Or are you committed to fulfilling your own destiny?* I didn't hear voices of old baseball players, but for the first time in a long time, I listened to my life instead of trying to control it.

You were not destined to be left in the dark about your life purpose or even your life work. When you ask honestly and with no qualifications, "it will be given to you"

(Matthew 7:7). For some reason, that asking can seem extremely difficult for most of us. Our pride stands in the way. Having faith in the area of career and calling may mean summoning the faith and courage to ask for help.

See God's Hand in Your Own History

The difficulties in the lives of great people marked them but in many ways made their greatest accomplishments possible. In the midst of agonizing odds and a tremendous beating from the continual bombings by Nazi airplanes, Winston Churchill inspired a nation to endure and "never, never, never give up." He came to the conviction that his life and his many heartaches and political dead ends served a purpose. He would later say, "I felt as if I were walking with destiny, and that all my past life had been a preparation for this hour and for this trial."[4]

Of course, you realize that winning such victories against the odds is what makes a hero. But as you face the future of your own calling, you will have to make a choice: to endure and recognize a hand that has been shaping you or to throw in the towel and see yourself as "floating around accidental-like with the wind."

As spiritual writer and twentieth-century monk Thomas Merton wrote, "all you really need is in your life already." Merton called this "hidden wholeness."[5] This means being willing to recognize that even the most horrific parts of your past had a purpose. "All things work together for the good," wrote Paul in Romans 8:23. Your painful heritage and life challenges can create a spiritual wisdom and resilience that prepares you for what's to come in this life and the next. Your opportunities and blessings may do the same.

One close friend of mine (Jeff's) wrestled with his background in a prominent public family. At times, he said, "it felt more like a whole lot of expectations I felt I needed to live up to." But he finally came to accept his birthright: "This is what I've been given. I can either keep trying to be something different or just see it as God's gift."

You weren't created and called to a destiny that you can never reach. You weren't born for frustration or called to mediocrity. Your circumstances aren't a cosmic joke and your destiny to sink into a ditch with a flat tire and no spare. Consider the experiences, gifts, or blessings from your past that may be the hand of God at work in your history.

So how do you look for spiritual clues from your past?

Your "Aha" Moments (*Chronos* vs. *Kairos*)

The Greeks used several words that correspond to the English word *time*. First, there's *chronos,* which can be defined as "measured time." It's the minute-by-minute and moment-by-moment experience of time. Some of us feel constrained by it. It makes us feel anxious. We try to manage it or control it. There never seems to be enough of it. And when it's gone, it's gone.

Another Greek word for time is *kairos,* which can be defined as the "fullness of time." It's the present, time without limit, the kind of time God inhabits: not dragged to the next thing or too busy to notice, fully there, alive to the now.

As it relates to how we work or operate, some have more recently described it as flow or possibly "aha" moments. This is when the lightbulb comes on inside, giving energy or even the answer to a confusing question.

While I (Jeff) was speaking to a superintendent of a large Illinois school district over breakfast, I shared my study of these two Greek words, *chronos* and *kairos.* Had he ever experienced a *kairos* moment?

He paused, then with intensity in his eyes, said, "Jeff, I would have to say it was the first time I taught a large group of people. I felt like I could do this forever!"

"Interesting," I said. "That's what you do best, Steve. You're a teacher."

Then he turned the question to me. "How about you Jeff? When have you experienced *kairos*?"

I paused for a moment. "What comes to mind was when I participated in a retreat held in Pennsylvania's Pocono Mountains in the 1970s. The facilitator invited each of us to write our own thoughts in a personal letter to God. Later that night I left everyone else and wandered out into the night to an open field. As I stared up into millions of stars, I felt God's presence in a way I never had before. It's very vivid, even now. And though I didn't hear any kind of audible voice, I clearly knew there was a message for me: 'Jeff, I created you for a reason. Your life has a purpose.'"

When I finished, Steve was nodding. "That makes a lot of sense," he said knowingly. "You write. Writing is an expression of your soul. It brings you peace. And you're all about fulfilling your purpose—and helping others fulfill theirs."

Since then I've asked many people this question. "When have you experienced *kairos*? When have you had a moment when time just seemed to stand still—you were fully present, fully alive?" The pattern in the way they respond is clear. Something pops into their mind, and it seems random. From deep inside they recall something that's fundamental to them. Their "aha" moment, a time when they sensed they were doing something that was fully them. It was life at its fullest, a spiritual moment.

Have you experienced a *kairos* or an "aha" moment? _____

When was it? _____

Where were you? _____

_____

What were you doing? _____

_____

Experience Spiritual Gifts

One of the hardest things for any of us to do is to determine what gifts are from God and what's just us trying hard. As you explore the spiritual nature of gifts, you will recognize that you must get down to the core of who you are and what you do best, not just what you like to do or think you should do.

The Bible teaching is quite clear in this matter. God has given certain gifts to use for others' benefit. The word in Greek, *charisma,* can directly be translated as "grace gifts" or "free favor" or as translated today, "spiritual gifts." God freely gave these to His people. Paul explains, "We have different gifts, according to the grace given us. If a man's gift is prophesying, let him use it in proportion to his faith. If it is serving, let him serve; if it is teaching, let him teach; if it is encouraging, let him encourage; if it is contributing to the needs of others, let him give generously; if it is leadership, let him govern diligently; if it is showing mercy, let him do it cheerfully" (Romans 12:6–8).

Now you need to find your own spiritual gifts. Here is a short list that will help you narrow them down.

Spiritual Gifts

This is in no way meant to be an extensive or definitive list of spiritual gifts. It is meant to awaken you to some of the possible ways that spiritual gifts may influence or affect your calling. You may be called to use these gifts full-time (or get paid for what you do) in some kind of vocational ministry position. Or these may enlighten you to a gift that you would want to use in volunteering or making an impact outside of your career.

The best way to detect a spiritual gift is to look into your past and identify an occasion in which you went beyond your natural abilities or skills. In the wake of what you did, you notice the effects, things you accomplished with a power greater than your own.

As you read over this list, think about which of these gifts sound like yours.

Entrepreneurial leadership (apostleship). Start new ministries or businesses to recruit and equip new leaders or provide expansion. Individuals with this gift often function as generalist leaders before bringing others with more focused gifts into their mission.

- I have been used by God to start things.
- I don't mind recruiting people to be part of things I believe in.
- I tend to be entrepreneurial.
- I have little trouble navigating in uncertain circumstances and don't mind not having a clear path laid out for me.
- I am more of a starter than a long-term manager.

Leadership. To guide or orchestrate other people in a sustained direction. Such individuals often build and direct a team to accomplish a spiritually significant purpose.

- I often influence or compel others toward a goal or vision.
- People tend to look to me for leadership.
- I tend to be self-confident when I really believe something.
- I am comfortable when others look to me for direction, guidance, or a plan.

Teaching. Building others up through introducing and explaining spiritual truth. Able to simplify what seems complex.

- I enjoy organizing and explaining things so that people seem to get it.
- I am especially apt to explain truth to others so that what seemed unclear becomes clear.
- People seem to apply the things I teach.

Evangelism. Ability to influence others toward faith and to explain God's good news. Such individuals communicate this message so that others actively respond.

- I am drawn into spiritual discussions with people.

- I naturally build relationships with people who don't have knowledge or are uninterested.
- I have a love and passion for helping others find ultimate hope.

Helping. Ability to work behind the scenes of an endeavor and attend to physical or task-oriented matters.

- I am attracted to behind-the-scenes work that others may not see.
- I don't mind getting my hands dirty.
- I prefer not to be in the spotlight.
- I often enjoy working alone or with others to accomplish necessary tasks.

Generous giving. Ability to give resources of money and property eagerly and abundantly and with strategic focus on God's work in the world.

- I get a deep joy from giving funds or material goods to those with real needs.
- I am sometimes moved by the needs I see and feel a genuine desire to help meet those needs—even if I do not receive recognition.
- I look for ways my resources can help others.

Hospitality. Creating a welcoming space for strangers and fostering the development of community among people.

- I enjoy doing things that make outsiders connect with others and feel welcome and important.
- I get energy by seeing people connect with each other and enjoy being together because of my efforts.
- I regularly seek out ways to help people meet and get to know each other.

Administration. Creating order and structure within and around a church, business, or mission; arranging and working with a detailed process so that it functions smoothly and in order.

- I am prone to creating order and organization.
- I enjoy planning and creating structures for people in the church.
- People tell me that things run smoothly when I organize them.

Encouragement. Able to evoke spiritual and emotional courage, faith, and action in a person or community.

- I tend to see in people positive traits and abilities they don't necessarily see in themselves.

- I authentically desire to inspire others to live up to their God-given potential.
- Others have told me that I inspire them to hope and be their best.
- I inspire others to do what they might not do on their own.

Shepherding. Nurturing and guiding others toward growth and maturity.

- I guide and nurture people outside my own family.
- Others come to me when they need someone to listen to them.
- I see untapped potential in others.

Faith. Ability to trust in God's provisions and promises personally and on behalf of others. Those with gifts of faith have an outstanding ability to withstand challenges without wavering and a desire to trust God for great things.

- Others tell me I have a courageous faith.
- I am especially confident that God will work things for the good in difficult circumstances.
- I feel fully alive when I am out on a limb of faith and trusting God with all my heart and seem especially enabled to do so.

List your top three spiritual gifts here:

1. _____
2. _____
3. _____

What Am I Passionate About?

A FEW DAYS after resigning my (Tom's) intense position as a vice president of sales, my whole relationship to work and career came to a crossroad. Because I finally had some time to think late that summer, I headed out for a long head-clearing hike with my golden retriever. Though I tried to relax, I couldn't get the thoughts about what to do next out of my head. As I continued along the wooded trail, I came to a split in the path. Ironically, it looked like a picture of my career decisions. Unclear, kind of confusing, diverse. *Do I take the well-defined road?* I asked myself. *Do I head out on the new path? Or do I try something completely different and blaze my own trail?* "God," I prayed, "what am I supposed to do next?"

> ## Chapter Take-Aways
> - Discover your passion by examining the high and low points in your past.
> - Understand what you're most passionate about in your career and in your personal life.
> - Find your passion in the categories of people, place, and action.

I stood there almost paralyzed by all my options. Then my legs just started moving into the woods. I headed into the thick underbrush and started blazing a new trail. My dog probably wondered if I had lost my mind. I began bushwhacking through trees, sticks, and endless brush. After what seemed like a whole lot of work, I came to a large clearing. It may sound like no big deal, but I felt like I had accomplished something! As the sun beat down on me, I realized this was my answer. It was time to do something different. This confusing fork was really my opportunity to go in my own direction and do what I really loved doing, coaching others to find jobs they could love. It became clear to me: it was time to start a company that would combine my skills as a businessman and recruiter with my passion to help those experiencing career transition. Although there have been ups and downs, I can honestly say I've never looked back.

Define Passion

Webster's dictionary defines *passion* as "compelling feeling or emotion; . . . a pursuit to which one is deeply devoted." Its synonyms include *love, ardent affection,* and *zeal.* The opposite of *passionate* is *passive:* "being without response to something, not active, inert." Unlike passive people, passionate people can't remain inactive or inert in the realm of their passion. They're compelled to action.

At its core, passion involves energy. Like a flame, it's a source of heat and light. Some relate this to what they call emotional intelligence; others to flow or being in the zone. Whatever the term, experts today realize that such emotional motivation can be even more important a factor in achieving success than IQ, education, or experience.

Think about some passionate people for a moment. Who comes to mind? We may think of public figures such as Martin Luther King Jr. They speak with intensity and charisma as they rally others to their cause. Some may think of Olympic hockey players who push themselves to the limit to win in overtime. They don't give up when things get tough or look bleak. Or there's the self-sacrificing passion of a Mother Teresa caring for a person with a painful disease, feeling the other's pain, and mercifully tending to their needs.

In the workplace passionate people provide the energy that gives meaning and the push to move beyond just getting stuff done or earning a paycheck. This includes people like Ed, who in retirement chooses to work the dawn shift at UPS because he wants to stay active and he "kind of enjoys" finding and fixing lost packages. And he does it at 4:00 A.M. each weekday. (Warning: doing this in your retirement without passion may be hazardous to your health!) Or there's Jill, the software company chief financial officer who pores through complex financial statements to keep the bottom line off the bottom. She too feels passionate about what she does and sees herself making a difference.

In his book *Halftime,* businessman and nonprofit founder Bob Buford asks, "What is your passion, the spark that needs only a little breeze to ignite into a raging fire?"[1]

If you know the feeling of passion, you know the image of a raging fire is an accurate one. Passion creates the heat and energy to fuel activity that may seem impossible to others. Passion brings you to the edge of your seat. It can cause you to pound the table in a meeting. Passion causes your heart to race or brings tears to your eyes. Such sincere emotions can be clues to your deepest and truest self if you pay attention.

Passion expresses itself in both the high and low points in your life. Some of the more intense emotions you experience come from hardship or disappointment. Steve Lake, who has a doctorate in education as well as being an expert in vocational discovery, calls this looking at your "stars and your scars."[2]

Actor Michael J. Fox seeks to help others find a cure for Parkinson's disease. Christopher Reeves fought to help those who sit in wheelchairs. Charles Colson, who was convicted and sent to prison after Watergate, leads a ministry to prisoners and their families.

Take the time to explore your passion. Get away from the urgencies and the emergencies of life to invest in looking back. Tom went to the woods behind his house. Jeff once piled ten years' worth of journals into his car and headed to the mountains of Vermont: "I holed up in little motel to search what I should do next. Admittedly, this felt like hard work in some ways . . . But as I hunted for clues, the voice of my own passion became clear. The decisions I made that day gave me the confidence to move ahead with a new venture."

So enough of the words! Let's get to work. What's your passion?

Discover Your Passion

It's likely that things have already started to come to mind for you. Here's a way to test for the presence of passion.

Top Ten Ways to Recognize It's a Passion

1. Your face turns red and you become animated when you talk about it.

2. You typically find yourself curious and seek to learn more about it.

3. You don't get tired when actively engaged with it.

4. You could stay up late talking about it or doing it and wonder where the time went.

5. You wouldn't need to get paid to invest time or energy in it.

6. Others seem interested in speaking with you about it.

7. You sometimes wonder why others aren't as passionate as you about it.

8. If you had a day off, you would enjoy engaging in it.

9. If you had all the money, time, and freedom in the world, you would be involved with it.

10. If you were in a bookstore, you might easily gravitate toward issues that relate to the topic of your passion.

Now that you've discovered some clues to your passion, it is to time to examine them more closely.

The Passion Finder

The benefit of being able to understand and articulate your passion at this time may save you years of trial and error. What's the cost of not knowing your passion now?

We believe it is scars and wasted time. It is the job you accepted for the wrong reasons, money without happiness, promotions with no satisfaction, burnout, not living the life you were designed to live, not contributing to the world what you can contribute.

For this reason the most significant thing you take from this book may be a clear understanding of your passion and a commitment to use it in your employment. No one else can help you find your passion. It's a private screening into your life. This doesn't mean that you won't need some helpful tools for your search. What follows may be the first tool you've ever used to paint a passion picture.

The focus of your passion can be broken down into three main subsets:

- **People:** a passion for working with or helping certain people
- **Place:** a passion to spend time or invest yourself in a location
- **Action:** a passion to do a type of work or activity most important to you

These subsets represent the who, where, and how of your passion. We've chosen a triangle to represent these three focuses of passion. The triangle represents the strength of equal proportions with a peak always at the top.

Try to pick your top passion for your career, according to the categories we have discussed. Remember that each of these (people, place, action) is going to be important, but one will stand out and belong at the top of the passion triangles you will create later in the chapter.

Passion

Look at the descriptions in Figure 3.1 to see which category best reflects your career passion.

FIGURE 3.1 Passion Triangles

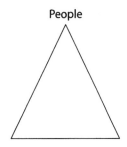

People

Who Will You Work With?
- Working with a certain kind of person.
- Helping people in a supporting role.
- Being part of a team.
- Valuing the people you work with more than the job.

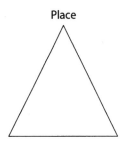

Place

Where Will You Work?
- Place you live in relationship to your job.
- Type of work environment: inside or outside, fast or slow pace, big or small company.
- Environment of the workplace: downtown, in the country, or in a small town.
- Location of the workplace: snowy Colorado, fast-paced New York, or sunny Florida.

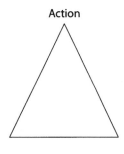

Action

What Will You Do?
- Type of job is key.
- Room for advancement to the top.
- Action situation.
- The kind of job is more important than where or with whom you work.

Now fill out Worksheet 3.1 to get some idea of how people, place, and action figure in your search for passion.

WORKSHEET 3.1

Identifying Your Passions

Instructions: In order to build your passion triangle, you need to narrow your focus to some specific topics. Go through each section and place checks by the things that you're passionate about.

After you have checked certain topics, select the top three in each grouping. Remember that passions are not just interests. They give you fulfillment and energy. Once you have picked three in each section, select from each area the one about which you have the most passion.

People: Who Will You Work With?

❏ Infants
❏ Young children
❏ Junior high school
❏ High school
❏ College students
❏ Poor or homeless
❏ Men
❏ Women
❏ Single adults
❏ Senior citizens

❏ Internationals
❏ Ethnic group
    (Which one?_____)
❏ Married couples
❏ Single mothers
❏ The wealthy
❏ Students
❏ The lonely
❏ People in crisis
❏ People in transition

❏ Leaders
❏ The addicted
❏ People needing motivation
❏ People with disabilities
❏ Anyone (a person is a person)
❏ Family
❏ Extended family
❏ Other_____

Of those that you have selected, which top three do you have a passion for?

Three Areas of Passion: People   Primary Passion: People

_____

_____   _____

_____

Place: Where Will You Work?

❏ Corporate settings
❏ Church
❏ Vacation settings
❏ The city
❏ The mountains
❏ The ocean
❏ The tropics
❏ Seasonal
❏ Abroad

❏ Third world
❏ Regular travel
❏ Near my family of origin
❏ Near my home
❏ Arts and cultural
❏ Medical
❏ Intellectual
❏ Religious
❏ Sports settings

❏ School or other campus
❏ My neighborhood
❏ Suburb of major city
❏ Rural
❏ Inner city
❏ Anywhere (not important)
❏ Other_____

Of those that you have selected, which top three do you have a passion for?

Three Areas of Passion: Place   Primary Passion: Place

_____

_____   _____

_____

Action: What Will You Do?

- ❏ Money management
- ❏ Personal development
- ❏ Education
- ❏ Entertaining
- ❏ Cultural issues
- ❏ Community service
- ❏ Environment
- ❏ Medicine or health
- ❏ Politics
- ❏ Scientific study
- ❏ Hospitality
- ❏ Justice

- ❏ Parenting
- ❏ Writing
- ❏ Public speaking
- ❏ Sports
- ❏ Travel
- ❏ Spiritual growth
- ❏ Organizations
- ❏ Creating or designing
- ❏ Engineering
- ❏ Counseling
- ❏ Study or reading
- ❏ Building

- ❏ Coaching
- ❏ Consulting
- ❏ Leading
- ❏ Entrepreneurial
- ❏ Technical
- ❏ Managing
- ❏ Physical labor
- ❏ Financial security
- ❏ Communicating
- ❏ Other_____

Of those that you have selected, which top three do you have a passion for?

Three Areas of Passion: Action   Primary Passion: Action

_____

_____   _____

_____

After identifying your three top passions, select the one true area (people, place, or action) and list the one passion that most represents you. For example, Jeff's top passion is in the people category, particularly working with leaders; Tom's primary passion is in the action category, particularly doing the work of leading.

Top Category:_____

Top Passion:_____

So Now What?

Now that you have identified your passions, ask yourself these questions: Are you there? Are you working or fully participating in your passion areas? Do your career and personal life align and balance each other out? If they're in alignment, that's great! If not, it's time to step back and look at your life and the changes you can make to intentionally combine your passion with what you do in your work. Shifting into higher gear is much easier when you realize that gear may free you to live out your passion.

CHAPTER 4

What Do I Value?

A S YOU CONSIDER your career, your values are not only important, they're essential. When you employ the largest block of your waking hours in activity consistent with your values, you feel whole and balanced. You get—not just give—energy.

I (Jeff) value service. I believe in it, teach about it, and look for it in others. I value it so much that I took time out of my schedule to attend a two-day conference on servant leadership in Cambridge, Massachusetts, that included speakers such as Ken Blanchard, Peter Drucker, and Bob Buford.

I came home from the conference just in time for dinner that night. I joined dinner already in progress with my wife and young children. Five-year-old Jonathan looked up at me and asked me where I had been and what I had learned.

> ### Chapter Take-Aways
>
> - Recognize the way your values are already shaping your everyday life and work.
> - Consciously detect and embrace your most important values.
> - Align your career choices with your chosen values and experience the freedom of living by what you believe is most important.

"Great question, Jonathan! We learned about what it means to be a servant."

"Daddy? What's a servant?"

"A servant is someone who helps other people. They see a person's need, and they do something to meet that need."

"Oh. Mommy? You're a servant."

"Why, thank you, Jonathan."

"You're always doing all kinds of stuff to help me and Jeffrey and Josh. And you too, Daddy!"

"Why, thank you, Jonathan!"

"Yeah, Daddy. Mommy's always serving *you!*"

We couldn't stop laughing, but the message was loud and clear: Daddy had some work to do to practice what he preached, at least around the house.

Our values (the ones we live and hold) act as our inner guidance system and drive the decisions we make. They're the internal price tag we put on activities, behaviors, and decisions. Webster's dictionary defines *value* as "assigned worth, valuation, significance or importance of a thing." It's what pulls us into action or pushes us to act or react when others around may not.

One of the main reasons I (Tom) named my company Integrity Recruiting & Consulting is because I truly value integrity in all that I do. Although I don't live this out perfectly, it is a value that drives me to do what I do daily. People have told me that using the words *integrity* and *recruiting* in the same phrase is an oxymoron, but I believe that integrity and recruiting can go hand in hand. That's a key part of my company's mission statement.

You may already have clear and defined values, or you may not have a full grip on your values. Even if they are things like "good food, good fun, and three-day weekends," these are values. What are yours?

The Bible teaches that God is a true picture of consistent values. For instance, God does not lie. He is a God of truth. His values and His being are one and the same. "I do not change like shifting shadows," God says (James 1:17 NIV). We can also tell a lot about God's values by what He does. For example, God exhibits the value of creativity by the beauty we see in the world. Think about it: Have you seen a tropical reef up close or on TV? Talk about variety and creativity!

Hyrum Smith, the creator of the Franklin Planner (schedule planner), put it this way, "And this simple concept, of making sure that our daily activities reflect our deepest core values, is the concept that has made all the difference in my own life."[1] What I do will reflect who I am. It can't do otherwise. So why not be intentional? We all want to be able to someday say, "I lived my life. Life didn't just live me!"

Notice Your Competing Value Voices

If you're old enough, you may remember the Tom and Jerry cartoons. Every once in a while, we'd see two angels speaking into the ear of Tom the cat, a good angel and bad angel (or devil). One would whisper, "Love your neighbor." The other, "Eat your neighbor." Though it's not always so easy to distinguish the good from the bad, most of us have competing values vying for our career attention.

Let's say you have a major life decision to make. You've been offered a unique job opportunity. They really want *you*. It's a golden opportunity and almost too good to believe! But there's a catch. You must make your decision in one hour, take it or leave it. Oh, there's one other catch: this position will take you to a distant city. You'll need to pack up your belongings, leave behind all that's familiar, and throw yourself into this venture, this opportunity of a lifetime.

How will you decide?

Your own reality TV host now enters the picture. "Good day," he tells you. "I've got some good news for you. You won't have to make this decision alone. Ten of your most influential advisers are here at their own expense to help you make the decision. This handful of folks will compete to gain your attention, then coach you with wisdom to ensure that you make right choice. Each one tells me they are committed to persuading you to do the right thing at all cost. And here they are!"

Which eager advisers enter your reality show? Your dad? Your mom? Your brother or sister? A past teacher? An old boss? An influential uncle? A trusted girlfriend?

Be careful about values that others see as imperative—your advisers may try to live them through you.

"But Mom, I really don't want to be a doctor."

"Sally, I don't want to hear another word about that. You have too much potential, and I won't see you throwing your life away like your big brother did! There are plenty of others who can work with special-needs kids. My father was a doctor, and Grandpa was a doctor, and now it's your turn. Please, honey, it would break my heart!"

On the other hand, it can be helpful to invite friends and family to act as sounding boards. They know us best. But don't forget, the final decision should be yours alone. "Dad, I've really been thinking and feeling called to the ministry, and although I know it's my choice, I wanted your input."

The first step to reconciling these competing voices (and the voices of friends and family) is to discover your true values. This can be difficult, but the following exercises should help.

Admit Your Values

A simple way to see what you currently value is to look at where you spend your time and money. The easy way to do this is to pull out your checkbook, your last few credit card statements, and your weekly planner (Figure 4.1).

Now look at the last three or four months. What filled your schedule? What you may see is all work and no play. This may show you that your personal life is withering away. Or you may see that you volunteered remodeling or repairing homes ten times over the last few months, and as you think about it, a smile comes to your face. Or maybe you worked at your daughter's school as a substitute teacher six times; each time you had the chance to spend quality time with your daughter. What we do (especially when we are on our own) most closely reflects what we value.

Of course, some values fall into a category of either right or wrong, black or white. We all want truth, justice, and love—not lying, injustice, and hate. We are looking for values more specific to you and your gifts and deepest needs here.

FIGURE 4.1 Checkbook and Weekly Planner

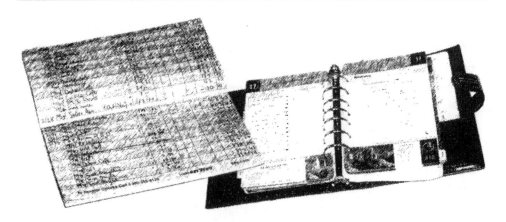

Sometimes your dreams can lead the way to your values. Be completely honest here:

Today is declared a holiday, and you can do whatever you want. What will you do?

What if next month is declared a holiday? What will you do?

What if you had all of next year off?

How did you respond? Your initial responses may alert you to a neglected or even dormant value. Maybe it's too hard to even answer. Those questions seem so improbable that you can't even begin to think that way. But if something's becoming clear, it may be a tug pulling on your heart and calling you to heed the clues to what you really value.

If that doesn't quite get at your values, look at money. Let's say you've just inherited a few million dollars from your rich uncle. Off the top of your head, what three things would you do with the money? Don't overthink this.

1. _____
2. _____
3. _____

Now think about your choices. What do they reveal?

Another way to gauge what you value is to look at your past spending habits. Where did the money all go? Of course, you had to pay for necessities, the fixed expenses. But what happened to the excess? Did you save or buy? What did you buy? What did you give away? What did you invest?

Take a look at your monthly budget and see if you have you enough for each month or are going further into debt. Is your home too expensive for your current job? Could you or would you be willing to downsize to a lower income if you were to be energized by your work? What kind of shift would you need to make?

The bottom line in this exercise is to consciously take note of where you spend your time, money, and energy. Are you happy with your choices, or would you make a change if you had the opportunity? It's time to shift into a higher gear.

Allocating Your Pie

Picture each day of your life as a pie. You allot each of your values a slice of a certain size. Some slices are not negotiable, such as time for sleeping, eating, and doing chores. For the most part, these slices still leave a lot of pie left over. If you're typical, a large slice of a day goes in the work category. Add these daily slices of pie together into a lifetime, and the largest piece of waking pie may just be your work or career. It's larger than your education, free time, or even time with family. You will likely spend over eighty thousand hours in your lifetime at work.

Now imagine you can't stand what you do. You feel stifled or stuck giving all that pie each day to your work. You don't care much about it and don't see it as much more than a means to a paycheck. Here's our question for you: Do you really believe that God has designed and called you to spend the largest chunk of your pie in something that drains or bores you or underuses your talents? Is it God's will that you be miserable most of the time? We think not! Don't bury your talents. Your gifts matter.

How would you feel about being the patient of a surgeon who really could take or leave medicine? Let's say that, if she could, she would get out of it in a heartbeat. Yes, she studied at Johns Hopkins and still has student loans to pay. She's even been written up in the *New England Journal of Medicine*. But she finds her work distasteful, often tedious, and wishes she hadn't given up her dream to be an actress. How would you like to be lying on the operating table when this bored surgeon reaches for her scalpel?

Contrast that with the person who allocates much of their pie to something they feel great about. They're passionate about their work and feel blessed they have the opportunity to do what they love. They merge their dearest values with their work. They feel energized, and it shows.

This looks more like a couple we know who decided, after clarifying their values, to postpone retirement. Together they determined to continue operating their financial business because they saw it as a way to use their generous income to support charitable causes. Another friend recognized that his most important values were adventure and nature. He left a corporate job in Boston, moved to Maine, and took a job as a whitewater rafting guide. Today he owns the company and even operates a live radio show from his remote location.

Which of these people is doing the right thing? All of them. The reason: they're harmonizing their pie with their priorities. They are living examples of value-based career decisions.

You have the same freedom to choose your path. You have the freedom to choose how you slice your pie today and tomorrow. No one else can or should make that choice for you. And when you align your truest values with what you do each day, watch out! You will find the energy and peace to accomplish more than you may have dreamed possible—without sacrificing your self-worth or core beliefs. You will feel in sync with how God has made you and with your own heart.

Now here comes a little bit of work that can create a *huge* reward. Be one of the few who really takes the time to think this through, then take the risk to change if need be. This may take a monumental leap of faith or just confirm what you're already doing. But please honor your life by proactively reflecting on your values. We've never heard of anyone on their deathbed say, "I only regret that I lived for what mattered most to me." Plenty of people have said just the opposite.

Are you ready to take the risk? You might want to start by answering the following two questions. Then we're going to invite you to go through a values exercise that will help you bring focus to this vital issue.

If money were no issue, what would you be doing now?

If you could do anything, and do it anywhere, what would it be?

House of Values

Building a house involves three distinct but interdependent basic steps. If you've ever built a house or watched one being built, you noticed a logical progression from one structure to the next.

1. The foundation supports the entire structure. The foundation provides the stability and the platform on which all the other pieces rest.
2. The walls give support and shape the house's quality and character. They provide the identity by which one home is distinct from another.

3. The roof protects the home from the elements and provides security. Once it becomes damaged or leaky, the rest of the home soon becomes vulnerable to intrusion and decay.

Think of this image of a house as a metaphor for your values and the way they support, shape, and protect your life. As any contractor knows, you can't build walls or a roof if you haven't created a secure foundation. In the same way, you can't have stable walls for long if you don't design and maintain an adequate roof.

Take a look at the following lists of values. We've arranged them by several categories: core (foundation), family and relationship (walls), and career and work (roof). We've provided definitions to help you select and define your values. Feel free to add others that we may not have included or select values from other categories that may apply more accurately within any of your three value levels.

Core Values (Foundation)

Core values are the ones on which the whole structure of your life rests. Choose your top three. This may take some work and reflection or even a discussion with a trusted friend or mentor, but take the time.

Integrity	Doing what is consistent and right, no matter what the cost
Faith	Trusting in God and in His plan for life even when it's difficult
Legacy	Leaving behind values and influence that will live on after I am gone
Wisdom	Living with accurate understanding and belief, always seeking what is good and true
Spirituality	Living in light of God's guiding presence and relying on prayer and other spiritual disciplines
Authenticity	Being free to express my truest self and offer my gifts, ideas, and beliefs with honesty and freedom
Service	Giving energy, resources, and time to meet the needs I see around me
Responsibility	Taking charge of what must be done and doing it with diligence and excellence
Ethics	Acting according to what is right, true, and best
Honesty	Speaking the truth and being unwilling to compromise or lie

Peacefulness	Living in serenity with others, with your life and its events out of your control
Joy	Being grateful, content, and positive in whatever circumstances come my way
Courage	Being willing to take risks and stand fast in the face of challenges or adversity
Adventure	Seeing life as full of new possibilities and being willing to take risks to truly live
Flexibility	Being open to the changes, possibilities, and curves in the road that come with life and relationships
Tolerance	Being free of judgment and condemnation of people and circumstances
Caring	Allowing the plight and needs of others to touch my heart and motivate my actions
Perseverance	Being determined not to quit or become weary and possessing the ability to see things through to the end
Patience	Bearing with and enduring things that may be challenging, keeping things in perspective
Generosity	Willingly supplying tangible resources to meet others' needs
Health	Investing to maximize my energy, strength, and longevity
Love	Sharing myself and the best I have to offer with others
Purpose	Living for what matters most to me and succeeding in living out my calling

My top three _____ _____ _____

My primary _____

Family and Relationship Values (Walls)

Family and relationship values are fundamentally about how you approach and interact with others. Choose your top three.

Quality time	Spending great moments together in deep connection or creative engagements
Affection	Loving others through physical touch and tender care and compassion

Diversity	Being around different kinds of people and getting to know their specific beliefs, needs, and culture
Cooperation	Working with a group of like-minded people to do more together than each can do separately
Community	Sharing a depth of knowing and being known by others over a long period of time
Friendship	Being committed to mutually beneficial relationships defined by companionship, understanding, and shared experiences
Location	Being with those I value most in a place we truly enjoy
Forgiveness	Actively letting go of grievances and seeking peace and unity among my key relationships
Nurturing	Caring for the needs of those who matter to me in body, soul, mind, and spirit
Fun	Enjoying great times together doing things that bring mutual joy, shared memories, and often laughter
Understanding	Putting myself in others' shoes
Security	Providing for the needs of those I care about
Harmony	Keeping my relationships free of complications and stress
Spontaneity	Being free to invest the time and energy to enjoy being with others when opportunities arise
Teaching	Walking alongside others to provide them with knowledge, assistance, and guidance
Trust	Opening my heart to let others in without erecting barriers
Contribution	Giving and being an active participant in life and relationships
Respect	Allowing others to make choices and decisions without controlling them
Mentoring	Equipping others to succeed physically, mentally, spiritually, or vocationally
Listening	Hearing more than words and discovering the meaning of what others are really saying
My top three	_____ _____ _____
My primary	_____

Career and Work Values (Roof)

These basic career values shape how we approach our work. Choose your top three.

Creativity	Producing original ideas and products
Enjoyment	Deriving pleasure and satisfaction from my work
Expertise	Being highly skilled and an authority in my field
Financial security	Ability to meet financial obligations and be sure of regular income
Independence	Being self-directed and free from the control or authority of others I must work for
Environment	Living and working in the location or geographical setting I love and enjoy
Prestige	Receiving social recognition for valuable achievements
Responsibility	Managing a process, being reliable, being someone others can count on
Financial achievement	Attaining financial independence or above average wealth
Impact	Making a difference in others' lives, being a change agent for others' benefit
Variety	Having opportunities to move around, do different things, interact with new people, and experience new challenges
Risk-taking	Finding the exhilaration of going against the odds or overcoming challenges
Entrepreneurship	Creating something unique and new, with potential for growth
Generosity	Being able to give freely of resources: money, talent, or property
Building things	Creating physical, material, or artistic objects
Competition	Experiencing the thrill and challenge of pursuing victories, accomplishments, and excellence in what I do
Team	Playing an important role with a group of motivated others going in the same direction

Servanthood	Helping meet the real needs of others in order to make a notable difference
Personal growth	Increasing in character, knowledge, or experience and being shaped into a better person by what I do
Individuality	Expressing my unique personality, talents, or creative contribution through my work
Leadership	Playing a role in envisioning, empowering, and overseeing the activity of others in a team or task and fulfilling a worthy goal
Physical labor	Working with my hands and energy to achieve tangible physical accomplishments

My top three _____ _____ _____

My primary _____

Building Your House of Values

Once you have identified three values in each category, narrow your list down to one value in each category. Then list your top three values in Figure 4.2.

Now that you've built your house of values, it's time to take the next step in the journey and further clarify your calling by discovering your skill set. Your values in combination with your skills will point you in the right direction.

FIGURE 4.2   My House of Values

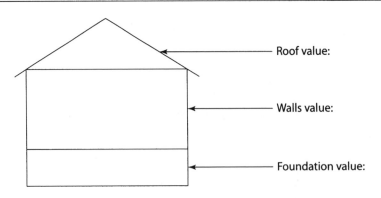

Roof value:

Walls value:

Foundation value:

CHAPTER 5

Know Your Skills

MOZART'S SKILLS as a composer and musician are legendary. From his youth his musical aptitude far surpassed that of his peers, including the fitfully jealous Salieri as portrayed in the movie *Amadeus.* Salieri could never measure up to the brilliant abilities of even the immature Wolfgang Mozart. No amount of practice, desire, or work could turn an average pianist and composer into a magnificent virtuoso.

In this chapter we will explore your natural skills. As you identify your natural skills, you can become an expert in your chosen field. We will also look at your trained skills, your transferable skills, and your innate or approach skills. We will break down and look at your past accomplishments that may lead or illuminate your marketable skills as well.

> ## Chapter Take-Aways
>
> - Create a list of your past accomplishments and understand their link to future achievements.
> - Review awards and recognitions that can help you set goals and prepare a résumé.
> - Identify your trained, transferable, and approach skills.

Webster's dictionary defines *skill* as "a developed proficiency or dexterity in some art, craft or the like." Now let's get to the bottom line of why this is so important. Your skills identify where you can plug in and excel. You can get paid for practicing your skills or make a contribution to society as a volunteer. What we want you to take away from this chapter is a clear understanding of the skills you've excelled at in the past and the skills you can confidently use in the future.

Accomplishments

In the investment world, mutual fund disclaimers highlight the fact that "past performance is not indicative of future results." However, when choosing to invest your hard-earned money and commit to a certain manager or mutual fund, wouldn't you want to know how the fund or investment performed over the past five or ten years? Of course. The past may not assure the future, but few would deny that they're related.

In the same way, your own past accomplishments do not guarantee future results in your career, and they don't assure success. Ask anyone who's made a soufflé, kicked a winning field goal, or made a huge sale. Nothing is guaranteed, but these accomplishments and experiences provide clues for future successes.

Now take the time to list five of your past accomplishments. Imagine Jay Leno holding a microphone before you onstage right at this moment. "Just off the top of your head," he asks, "what are five things you've accomplished in your life?" Or if Jay Leno seems like too much of a stretch, picture telling your very best friend, a career counselor, or someone you really trust.

My Accomplishments

1. _____
2. _____
3. _____
4. _____
5. _____

Now examine this list. Do you see some patterns or common themes? Underlying these accomplishments are the skills you attained and used. You did something with energy and direction. You feel good about it.

What do you notice?

Awards or Recognition

This can be a great, sad, or even touchy subject. But if you have won awards in the past, there was a reason for them. Remembering them also gives you clues to what you were great at in the past. This may also apply to how you craft a résumé when we look at this in Chapter Eight.

Awards certainly include trophies and public recognition for achievements. But the category may also include less public or glamorous recognition, such as getting an A in a class or on a paper. Or it may have involved certain promotions or even financial rewards.

Now list two or three awards or recognition you've received.

My Awards or Recognition

1. _____
2. _____
3. _____

Affirmations: "I See This in You"

Some people in our lives have seemed to know things about us that we didn't even notice ourselves. You look out of your own eyes and experience the world from inside you. You can't see yourself living; you're just living. Of course, every once in a while you can watch a video on which you appear or listen to a tape and think, *There's no way I sound like that!* But others sometimes see things in you that are important to know: "You're often late for our meetings." Or they see the positive side, "You're an amazing listener." "You show a lot of compassion to people in pain." "You think way outside the box and offer great ideas."

I (Tom) remember some key people who affirmed things they saw in me. As a child I regularly doubted that I could accomplish anything worthwhile. I was shy, a somewhat physically challenged kid with learning disabilities. One fifth-grade bully gave me the nickname Crooked Head. Fortunately, it didn't stick for long, but it made me wonder if my destiny was to be laughed at.

All this began to change one day when my high school football coach, George Parthemore, came to me after practice with a message. "Tom," he said, "you bring leadership skills to your teammates. I've seen this by the way you motivate them. They follow you, and they respond to your intensity." *Wow!* I thought, *if Coach Parthemore believes those things, maybe it's true!* You'd think I would have gotten this message, but by the time I entered the business arena, I was feeling that same insecurity. Again someone who believed in me reassured me. My new boss at the time, Dan Mathews, pulled me into his office and shared, "Tom, you're a terrific leader, and I think you

TABLE 5.1   Who Believed in You and Why?

Name	Their Role	What Did They Praise You For?	How Did You Feel?

have the skills to really make an impact." *Huh*, I thought to myself. *There it is again: leadership, working with a team. Might this be a clue to what I'm good at?*

How about you? You too may have had people in your past who affirmed strengths or even noticed things you hadn't noticed in yourself. Who were these people in your life? What did they see? Write your responses out in Table 5.1.

Seek input by e-mailing or calling some of these trusted people from either your past or present. You might be surprised by their response and their appreciation of your confidence in their feedback. Ask them the following questions:

- What skills do you see in me and why? (By *skills* I mean where you've seen me plug in and excel.)
- When did you notice me doing this?
- When you think of me, where do you see my skills best used?
- Finish this sentence: "Others have benefited from you because of your ability to . . ."
- What three adjectives best describe me?

We hope this confirmed what you already knew. Or perhaps it gave you new insight or encouragement to use or more fully develop these skills.

Your At-Work Skills

Now that you have looked at yourself through others' eyes, it's time to look in the mirror and evaluate how your skills manifest themselves at work. For example, some people possess skills that enable them to move things. Other people's skills enable them to move people. At-work skills are the tools you use to bring about change, build people or things, or influence outcomes in your work environment. You may have many such skills or just a few. This exercise will help you identify the ones you possess.

Job or Career Skills

What have you done before? What does your résumé say you have skills in? What skills have you gained through different experiences in jobs, volunteering, or education? Here are some examples of job or career skills:

Entering data	Creating training programs	Filing and organizing
Repairing computers	Acting	Teaching math
Managing projects	Balancing budgets	Setting up a clean room
Creating action plans	Repairing engines	Designing floor plans
Selling office supplies	Recruiting people	Driving semis
Driving forklifts	Doing telephone sales	Delivering mail
Preparing presentations	Leading teams	Preparing French food
Developing people	Giving speeches	Developing film
Writing copy	Researching on the Internet	Figuring formulas

Now take the time to select your three strongest job or career skills from this list or add something that's not there. These skills should involve activities or functions you have done in the past. You might want to look over your résumé or think of jobs or volunteer situations in which you've used these skills.

My Job or Career Skills

1. _____
2. _____
3. _____

Transferable Skills

Transferable skills are skills that can interrelate in different types of jobs or functions. For example, if you are a salesperson selling office supplies or insurance, your transferable skill would be selling. If you organize projects, your transferable skill could be managing projects.

Following are some transferable skills you might possess. Look through this list and circle ten in which you have the most skill. If you don't see one of your skills listed, add it to the list.

Dancing	Coaching people	Communicating
Writing	Helping others	Building things
Managing money	Hosting	Negotiating
Achieving sales results	Painting	Speaking in public
Putting things together	Delegating	Running meetings
Selling	Planning	Handling complaints
Working with details	Writing procedures	Encouraging others
Repairing things	Recruiting people	Operating machines
Completing inventories	Working with numbers	Inspecting products
Operating vehicles	Persuading others	Using mechanical skills
Inventing	Comparing data	Organizing
Comprehending	Creating	Improving things
Developing new ideas	Interviewing	Starting businesses
Using physical strength	Filing information	Coordinating
Recalling information	Teaching	Inspecting
Composing	Caring for others	Scheduling
Thinking practically	Working with tools	Solving problems
Arranging functions	Using logic	Editing information
Working in nature	Advising	Drawing
Using telephone skills	Confronting	Diplomacy
Designing	Using theories	Recording data

Doing precise work	Keeping financial records	Computing
Analyzing	Mediating	Using imagination
Being efficient	Being tactful	Expressing
Physical coordination	Servicing equipment	Calculating
Visualizing	Routine functions	Investigating
Using my hands	Purchasing	Initiating new tasks
Finding information	Classifying information	Customer service
Taking risks effectively	Following directions	Performing athletically
Playing music	Auditing information	Creating art or design

Once you have identified your top ten transferable skills, narrow the list down to five or fewer.

My Top Transferable Skills

1. _____
2. _____
3. _____
4. _____
5. _____

Approach Skills

Approach skills indicate the manner in which you will do your job, no matter what it is. These skills arise from your character or possibly from your core motivations or even convictions.

Following are thirty approach skills from which to pick. Circle your top six approach skills.

Flexible	Organized	Tactful
Calm	Responsible	Honest
Discreet	Neat	Cooperative
Efficient	Trustworthy	Positive

Dependable	Motivated	Punctual
Self-motivated	Sincere	Self-confident
Dedicated	Loyal	Persevering
Reliable	Hardworking	Willing to learn
Helpful	Encouraging	Open-minded
Mature	Industrious	Friendly

Now that you have found your top six approach skills, narrow them down to your top three.

My Top Approach Skills

1. _____
2. _____
3. _____

Now that you know your skills, what do you do with that knowledge? Be encouraged. You've been given these abilities to use directly or to help others. Don't take that lightly.

CHAPTER 6

What Are Your Interests?

I N BIBLICAL TIMES twelve men sailing in a boat on the Sea of Galilee in northern Israel observed something extraordinary. Out on the horizon loomed something they first thought was a phantom. The Scriptures record, "They were terrified" and "cried out in fear" (Matthew 14:26). Put yourself in that boat that stormy night. What would you have done next? What would you have said next? Eleven men did what most of us probably would have said and done: they gasped and stood speechless, completely flabbergasted. But one man did something different. He became curious and took action.

> ## Chapter Take-Aways
>
> - Clearly define your interests and areas for exploration.
> - Determine which interests are potential career paths and which are not.
> - Lay out the roles and activities to put your interests into your everyday work life.

As the title of John Ortberg's book reads, "If you want to walk on water, you've got to get out of the boat."[1] Twelve men witnessed a miracle because Peter's curiosity pushed him to get out of that boat.

What is it that leads some people to do what they do? They leap into action when an event, opportunity, or problem occurs. They focus all their attention on solving a problem. On any given workday, you'll find scientists in laboratories filling test tubes with fluid in order to discover a cure for a disease. Other people attend seminars to learn about sales techniques to help them sell their products and achieve profitable results. There are even people paid to drink coffee all day to determine the best mix or flavor that may create a new wave of interested coffee drinkers. All these people have one thing in common: they are curious about their field and want to know more.

Some career interests start off as hobbies or pastimes. They may grow into a full-time career or a steady stream of income. Dan, who grew up loving the stock market and read the *Wall Street Journal* from the time he was in junior high, now makes a living helping others with their investment needs. On the other hand, one of your interests that started as a pastime or hobby may remain just that. Jeff plays the guitar. Tom carves wood and ties flies for fly-fishing. We've never made a single dollar from these interests, but we enjoy doing them.

When you're thinking about your calling and career, pay attention to your interests. Some of the same curiosity that drags you into the elements or off the couch for fun may be the same propulsion that keeps you going day in and day out, late night after late night. Some of your interests may have developed from experience. You grew up around boats and the sea. You lived on a farm. Your father was an electrician. Your mom wrote books. Those who connect their interests and their career path get to "follow their inner light." They get to do who and what they are.

You may be saying, "There are too many things I'm interested in. How do I narrow it down?" In a universe of endless options, choices, and paths, how do you limit the field with any degree of confidence that you're not removing the nugget of gold as you sift the sand of options? In this case you need the challenge to make a decision. Or you may not know what's out there. There may be a calling and career you've never encountered that would fit you hand in glove. In this case you just need information. Or perhaps you know your interest quite clearly, but you've never seen the connection to career and calling. In this case you just need coaching—and possibly courage to make a change.

The Interest Flowchart

Most individuals who connect their calling and career go through a process or flow. Some do it consciously; most do it more unconsciously. It's time to experience the power and possibilities that may unfold as you decide to connect your interest more directly to your work.

For this reason we created the interest flowchart (Figure 6.1). It depicts the process of linking your interests to your career. It starts with this simple question: What am I interested in?

Now let's break the process down.

FIGURE 6.1   Interest Flowchart

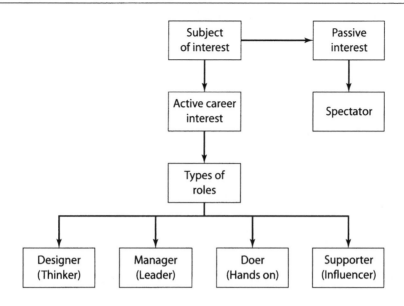

Subject of Interest: Who or What?

The subject of your interest is the person, process, or thing you focus on. It is your answer to the question: Who or what am I attracted to? Given the free time or the resources, what do I gravitate toward?

Think back to your own childhood for a moment. Consider third grade. It's a school day and you're in class. Your teacher announces, "Guess what class? It's recess time!" It's probably not difficult to remember what came next. The doors open and you get to choose your interest. Some children dash to the swingsets. Others clump into groups and begin to play a game of tag. Others run to the kickball field. How about you? Given the free time and the wide variety of options, where did you gravitate? What, or whom, were you attracted to? You understand the point. As we get older, it's the free weekend or the vacation. Given the freedom and variety, where do you focus?

The subject of your interest is like the piece of metal that attracts the magnet of your mind. The level of this attraction may vary according to your experience or even your personality. It may be a casual curiosity all the way to downright obsession, with many levels in between.

You may or may not be a student of your own interests. But you do possess enough interest to have read this far in this book. You care enough to invest time and energy in this search. So take a few moments to recognize your interests.

What subjects, objects, or activities interest you? Your answer may be a noun: art, politics, or computers. Or it may be a verb: designing, communicating, building, caring. It may be a person or place: ethnic groups, people with disabilities, children, Yellowstone, New York City.

Stop for a moment and think about this. Close the book if you have to and do this exercise. It should only take a few minutes. Don't overthink this. Keep it simple.

Brainstorm: What are your interests?

Of these, choose the top three and write them in the following list:

My Subjects of Interest
    1. _____
    2. _____
    3 _____

Pastime or Career?

Now consider each interest you just listed for a moment. Are these passive interests or active interests? By *passive,* we mean that this is something you have an interest in but not so much that you would make it a career orientation. You may want to read about, investigate, or enjoy these interests, but you're probably not going to attain a salary in this area. You may be short, slow, unable to hit a jump shot, and love to play basketball, but good luck making it in the draft! Or maybe you're really interested in fiction and own every Grisham novel ever written; but you don't write, edit, or publish—you read.

On the other hand, some interests elicit actions. For example, you're interested in furniture. You may craft furniture by hand in your basement shop. You may design furniture using pencil and sketch board. You may refinish the furniture you discover at small-town antique shows. Maybe you sell furniture in a mall showroom or buy furniture to outfit five-star hotels and upscale restaurants. The subject of your interest is the same in all of these. The actions are quite diverse.

FIGURE 6.2   Pastime or Career?

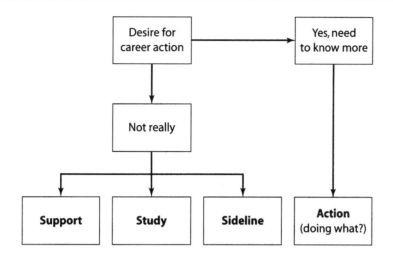

Which of the subjects of interest you listed are probably more spectator or hobby interests (at least at this point in your life)? Which of your interests would (or could) fall in the active area if you developed your skills, given some opportunity or effort? Figure 6.2 can help you decide which type of interest you have.

Action: Doing What?

What you do when you participate in your subjects of interest makes a big difference. Many people share an interest in medicine, but only some want to hold a scalpel and do surgery. Others with an interest in medicine would much rather do research, unlocking the key to discover a cure for cancer, AIDS, or heart disease. Others work one-on-one with patients to diagnose illness and treat the sick or troubled.

It's true that you may need to experiment before you land at exactly what you want to do with your interest, especially if you're just starting out. You may get involved with your field of interest and learn that you gravitate toward one action and away from another. You love to edit but really don't enjoy facing the blank page and writing. You could easily lead a team of writers as part of a publishing venture, but you feel drained when you produce your own original copy.

So think about what you do about your interest.

Role: Doing It How?

The action you take in relation to your interest also depends on the role you adopt or may adopt in the future. If you go back to the very first chapter, we discussed the idea that your past holds clues to your future and contains moments that define you. Though things may have changed significantly in your environment, your body, and your base of knowledge, some things haven't changed much at all. You're still the same you. Though it's no longer kickball, tag, or comic books, if you take the time to reflect you notice the same interest, paths, and tendencies at work.

We are all made for different roles. Once you choose your interest, you play a distinct role within that area or subject of interest. There are four unique roles you can play:

- Designer
- Manager
- Doer
- Supporter

The designer applies creative thinking, vision, or concepts to an area of interest that will grab other people's attention. Designers come up with ways to invent, sell, market, or enhance.

The manager gets thing done through others and leads the process of development within the interest area.

The doer gets his or her hands dirty in the actual stuff. Doers feel tugged toward the front lines and like to be in the action.

The supporter enables the other functions to complete their tasks. Supporters gravitate toward service behind the scenes and aid in organizations, causes, and endeavors.

Let's take a closer look at these roles. Been to Starbucks lately? Is the interest coffee, lattes, or cappuccino? In fact, it's really retail sales. Ultimately, the company is interested in profits for its stockholders.

This retailing interest includes all four roles.

The Starbucks designers mostly work in Seattle, the corporate headquarters. They create images, logos, and new products. They aim to create the ultimate coffee experience that sells around the world.

The Starbucks managers in the local café hire the employees and oversee their work. They handle the scheduling, ordering, and customer service and ultimately the profit generation for that location.

The doers at Starbucks have their own special title: baristas. These connoisseurs brew coffee, cappuccino, and espresso and serve customers.

The Starbucks supporters work behind the scenes. They ensure that cappuccino machines and cash registers work properly. They deliver the products designed by designers to locations managed by managers, where products are sold by doers to customers around the world.

Your fit may be one of these four or a combination of them. For example, you may be a designer who likes to do as well. Or you may be a manager who likes to support the doers behind the scenes as well as managing them. Or you may take one role with one interest and another role with a different interest.

Putting It All Together: Your Interest Flowchart

Take time now to sift through your interests as they relate to areas that draw you, the fields of interests that attract your curiosity, and write them out in the flowchart (Worksheet 6.1). Try not to overthink this exercise. Think globally and then whittle it down. A wood carver examines a piece of wood and visualizes a work of art inside. We now invite you to examine what inspires your own interests. Where do you see art that others do not?

Now that you've filled out the flowchart, you've taken the first step in identifying the interests you have a calling toward. It's time to shift into higher gear and explore these interests at a deeper level. As you discover your strengths and consistently combine them with your interests and skills, you will be drawn toward more fulfillment in your career. If you're looking for ideas, Chapter Ten will give you some ideas of how to find information about jobs in the library and on the Internet.

My Interest Flowchart

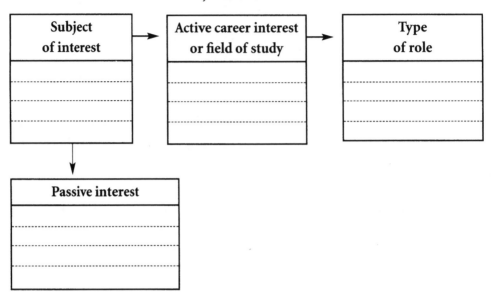

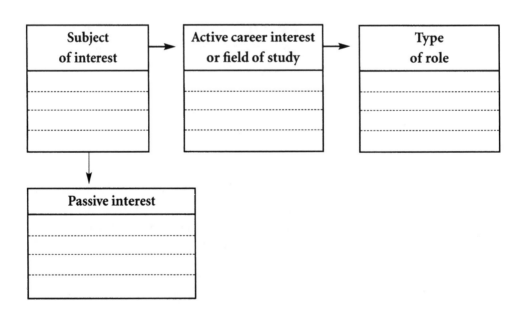

CHAPTER 7

Reality Check

AIRPLANE PILOTS DESCRIBE a phenomenon known as vertigo: the feeling and belief that one is flying right side up, when in actuality, the plane is flying upside down. "It's absolutely confusing," according to an air force pilot. "What you experience is a sensation of the sky up there, the earth down there. Then you look at your instruments— and they say, 'No, its actually the other way around.' If you don't change, you could be in serious trouble."

Like the pilot navigating the horizon who experiences vertigo, times of career change have the potential to throw off judgement or get our self-image out of whack. Some get tunnel vision and see only the new adventure or the possibility of glory. They underestimate the costs required and only see the benefits on the horizon. It's possible to underestimate how much money we really do need to meet our expenses or continue our lifestyle. On the other extreme, it's possible to let money become the all-important factor in our decision.

> ## Chapter Take-Aways
>
> - Have a firm grasp on how much risk you are willing to take by completing a risk survey.
> - Complete a monthly budget to understand your income needs.
> - Within two pages have a complete understanding of the keys to your calling.
> - Design an action plan to start living your career calling.

In this chapter we invite you to scan your gauges and perform your own reality check. Before preparing to embark on a new venture or leave your current situation, you may need to read instruments, or check messages from ground control (that is, spouse, family, close friends, others who know you best). Like a pilot preparing for a flight, you'll need a reality check to ensure that all systems are go and you've left nothing undone before takeoff.

Now right up front, we'll tell you that this process is not meant to pour cold water on the fire burning inside you. It's not nagging voice to say, "You can't do it!" The goal of a reality check is to make sure all systems are go and things that don't need to be left to chance aren't.

The first reality check starts very personally with you. It's your own spiritual sense of well-being. Of course, when examining the state of your soul, prayer isn't a bad place to start. The often quoted Lord's prayer says, "Thy will be done on earth as it is in heaven." If you really believe there's a larger purpose for your life, then are you open to engaging that "will on earth"? Can you say "yes. I'm open," hands open with no "unlesses" inserted? Yes, this takes faith and courage.

The second personal reality check involves another section of that same prayer. "Give us this day our daily bread . . ." It's dependence and even humilty. We recognize we weren't created to be "human doings," but admit, "I too am a human being." I require daily sustenance, provision, and I'm just like others. I don't need to prove I'm somebody by my title, any kind of recognition, or net worth. I don't "win" by doing special things to prove I'm a someone to anyone. If I'm called to work that's viewed as valuable by the masses, that's good. If I'm called to a vocation or position that's invisible and undervalued, there may be a reason that we may not fully comprehend for some time.

We'll be first to admit this kind of acceptance isn't easy. Both of us have worn "titles" with pride and felt like failures because of the car we drove or the house we lived in. We struggle with volatile self-images and compare ourselves with others. That's the truth. Yes, we're not proud of that—but when all is said and done, being at peace with who we are and doing things for the right reason matters most to us.

So as you start your reality check, would you stop for a moment and answer these two questions . . . or even pray these prayers.

1. Can I honestly say, "Thy will be done." "I am available."?

2. Do I believe I don't need to prove anything? I am content and pray "Give me this day my daily bread."

If you answered "yes" to these, you're in a great space and a great place. Way to go! Now, move on to some other reality checks.

Now comes the timing. Given what you've learned, is the way blocked or closed? Is the answer to your prayers saying "no"? Or, just the oppostite, is it a "go!"? Get ready and move out! Or is the timing wrong? Is this more of a "slow"?

Is this the time to reach for the stars, or should you methodically prepare and take one more step in a positive direction? This is not to say that if God is clearly calling you, He will not empower and equip you for what He has in store. Clearly, many would have challenged visionaries such as Thomas Edison, the Wright brothers, and Mother Teresa to keep their feet on the ground and their hearts inside their sleeves.

But what is the right amount of risk for you? Too much risk and you may lose everything. Not enough risk and you may be burying the very talents and potential you have discovered or more clearly defined in earlier chapters.

Before you shift into the next gear, we want you to invest in your own reality check so that you protect yourself and your loved ones and you don't crash and burn.

Define Your Risk Tolerance

Just as the pilot must check all gauges prior to takeoff, investors must gauge their risk tolerance before investing their money. Few could argue with the upside potential of certain investment opportunities. How much can an investment decline before the loss is just too great for the investor to bear, financially or emotionally? How many nights of sleep can the investor bear to lose if the investment heads south?

How much risk is right to take when it comes to your calling and career? The answer: it depends on you.

First, it depends on how you're wired and how much loss you can recover from and move on if this career, job, or venture doesn't work out. Your own peace of mind matters, and your ability to sleep well is something only you can put a price tag on.

Second, it depends on your season of life. It may be the most responsible thing for one investor to put up $5,000 toward a stock's initial public offering; but for someone else, it may be completely foolish and unrealistic. If the second person were to lose the money, it could devastate their home, their family, or their peace of mind. The same wise writer of Ecclesiastes who wrote, "Cast your bread upon the waters" (11:1) also wrote "There is a time for everything, and a season for every activity under heaven . . . a time to plant and a time to uproot . . . a time to scatter stones and a time to gather them" (3:1, 2, 5). Some seasons of life are more appropriate for certain levels of risk than others. Which season are you in now?

Third, it depends on what God is or isn't calling you to do. God invited Abraham to leave the harbor of his homeland and head into "a land I will show you" Genesis (12:1) NIV. Jonah was asked to stay away from a harbor and instead head inland to the corrupt city of Nineveh. In the book of Jeremiah (29:5), we learn that God commanded the ancient Israelites who were viciously carried into captivity in Babylon to settle: "Build houses and settle down; plant gardens and eat what they produce." They were told not to listen to the "prophets and diviners" who were encouraging them to dream: "'They are prophesying lies to you in my name. I have not sent them,' declares the Lord" (29:9).

Take the time to assess your risk tolerance at this juncture of your life by filling out Worksheet 7.1.

WORKSHEET 7.1

Risk Tolerance Test

Instructions: Complete the following test to evaluate your risk tolerance (Answer between 1–5, 1 being not very risk tolerant and 5 very risk tolerant).

I am willing to make changes in my life to live my calling.	1	2	3	4	5
Although money is important to me, I would rather follow my true calling even if I must pay a price.	1	2	3	4	5
I am willing to take chances with limited information.	1	2	3	4	5
When I look at my career calling, I'm not worried.	1	2	3	4	5
What I do is more important to me than how much I make.	1	2	3	4	5
I see my career calling as a journey, not a destination.	1	2	3	4	5
I have looked at the pros and cons of living my calling.	1	2	3	4	5
I want to be remembered for what I did and how than for having comfort or fame.	1	2	3	4	5

Now total your score from these questions and look at the key. Your score: _____

Key

35–40	Very willing to take risks.
29–34	Moderate.
24–28	Conservative.
19–23	Need to think more about it.
1–18	Stop reading this book.

Now that you've taken the test, you should be aware of where you stand. Your risk tolerance may be different or lower than you expected if you haven't gotten in touch with your career calling. Uncertainty can cause doubts where confidence should reign. The point is to recognize how you view risk right now, realizing that this may change over time as your career changes and as you change.

Recognize Your Prior Commitments

Prior commitments demand your time, attention, and money in ways that may preclude other possibilities. Let's face it, everything can seem to be in order, ducks all in a row, but one vital factor may stand in the way: a prior commitment.

You need to be willing to walk away from some of your prior commitments. You may need to leave behind the misfit occupation, the degree that's really just a diploma, or even the notoriety or status position or title. We know how humbling that can be because we've both been there.

But some other prior commitments may cause you to hit the pause button and possibly even to stop. These may require more discernment and some direct attention before you move forward.

Mike and Peg delayed a move across the country to care for Peg's ailing elderly father. When Grandpa Hickey passed away a few years later, they no longer felt attached to staying in snowy Buffalo. So when Mike was offered a cancer research position in Phoenix, he and Peg packed their bags and headed out. "I could get used to this," said Peg on a January day when the temperature hit 80 degrees.

Others make career decisions in relation to their children. Those decisions are typically the most confusing: filled with potential family guilt, peer pressure, and stereotypes of what a good mom or dad should or shouldn't do, Tricia postponed the possibility of becoming a partner in her law firm in order to focus attention on her newborn son. Jeff's brother Todd declined an invitation to run for Congress in his New Jersey district in order to spend more time with his six-year-old daughter. "I don't want to have to choose between a meeting in Washington and Sarah Kate's ballet recital," he said.

In the movie *It's a Wonderful Life*, George Bailey's brother, Harry, leaves behind his hometown to seek adventure and wealth in the military and in the big city. You know the rest of the story. George, hoping to "lasso the moon" in big business himself, instead makes one decision after another based on prior commitments.

George stays behind in Pottersville when his father dies. He steps up to the plate to help the troubled Bailey Savings and Loan and fight the corrupt intentions of Mr. Potter's dark power. George views himself as a failure, the brother who lost out. But through the eyes of an angel and Christmas magic, brother Harry, surrounded by a town of grateful people, proclaims, "This is my brother, George. The richest man in town."[1]

In the quiet of your own life, you may need to pray over and evaluate this one. Do your children need you right now? Will taking a job involving excessive travel or pressure hinder your life with family and friends?

"Daddy, I'm ready to go to cub scouts."
"Oh, nuts! I was planning on watching Monday night football with the guys!"

"Honey, will you please fix the furnace. It's smoking, and it's below zero outside."
"I can't right now, dear. I'm reading the last few chapters of an amazing novel. I'll take care of it next weekend."

"Ma'am, please help me. I feel like I'm going to pass out. I need my inhaler."
"I can't right now, miss, I really have to be on time for my aerobics class. Let me give you my cell phone. Call me in about an hour."

OK, so those scenarios are a bit extreme, but you get the point. There are times when prior commitments come before wants, desires, or even incredible opportunities. You may just realize that by investing in these prior commitments, you receive tenfold in return. You may have to actually downshift before you can shift into higher gear.

I (Tom) deal with this often in recruiting candidates for positions that require moving to a different location. The most difficult conversation is when I need to ask the candidate to speak with their family about the reality of a possible relocation or a new set of responsibilities. "Is everybody on board? Really?"

The question for you is: Do you have a prior commitment (or commitments) you must weigh as you look at this career calling? If yes, what is it? And how long will it last?

Understand Your Financial Needs

Some find that considering the money issue as it relates to calling and career is quite natural. Quotas, commissions, and financial packages go hand in hand with the job. Others have a more difficult time linking the two. They do their work for the love of it, and money is not the primary motivation. You don't get the sense that Mother Teresa ever asked, "What's the salary for the position in Calcutta? Do they offer a 401(k)?"

Some callings generate abundant income and are rewarded with perks and benefits. Others aren't rewarded much at all, at least monetarily. Their rewards aren't as easily quantifiable but may include the ability to provide job security, obtain a steady paycheck, earn goodwill, or gain the immeasurable benefit of knowing you're doing what you're supposed to do. As the credit card commercial puts it, "Priceless!"

So the real question for you to ponder is this: How much is enough? How much is enough to care for your prior commitments? How much is enough to fund your present and future priorities—a mortgage, an education, a wedding, a vision of retirement?

On the other hand, if the job is not in your area of strengths, gifts, or calling, the question is: How much money is it worth to experience the drain and pressure of working at a job that doesn't fit and in which you feel subtly inadequate?

Money has been called the root of all kinds of evil. Like a sharp knife in the hands of a toddler, it may pose grave danger to one not properly equipped. But it's also a tool to enable you to support yourself, your family, and possibly others while you do what you do best. And don't apologize for charging for your services or seeking to support yourself and your family by using your gifts.

The other reality check as it relates to money is this: How consistent does the flow of money need to be? Can you live with an inconsistent stream of income, or do you need a steady flow—for your and your family's peace of mind, for your financial responsibilities?

How much money do you need?

How much money do you want?

In Worksheet 7.2 we have provided a spot for you to complete a current budget that may help you answer these questions. This isn't a book about financial planning, but figuring out your financial reality can help you make informed changes.

Monthly Budget

Housing
    Rent   _____
    Mortgage (principal and interest) _____
    Real estate taxes   _____

Utilities/misc.
    Gas   _____
    Electric   _____
    Water   _____
    Cable   _____
    Garbage   _____

Insurances
    Auto   _____
    Life   _____
    Health   _____
    Disability   _____
    Long-term care   _____
    Homeowners   _____

Loans
    Autos   _____
    School   _____
    Other   _____

Current monthly expenses $ _____
Current monthly income $ _____
Difference $ _____

Telephone
    Home   _____
    Cell   _____

Credit cards
    1.   _____
    2.   _____
    3.   _____

Savings—Retirement
    Regular   _____
    College   _____

Tithe   _____

Food   _____

Auto expense
    Gas   _____
    Maintenance   _____

Spending   _____

Clothes   _____

Entertainment   _____

Home maintenance   _____

Medical expenses   _____

Misc.   _____

To live my calling, I'm willing to reduce my expenses in the following areas:

Area or Items to Reduce	Action(s) Required	Dollars of Savings

Total savings $ _____

Know Your Complements

Consultant and author Ralph Mattson works with groups of people to help them discover their role and the role of what he terms their "complement" (R. Mattson, pers. comm.). The whole idea of a complement harks back to the Garden of Eden, when God noticed the man He created, Adam, was incomplete. He remarked, "It is not good for man to be alone" (Genesis 2:18a NIV). It wasn't that Adam was flawed, unacceptable, or incapable. Yet he was unable to fulfill his God-given potential. He needed help.

God's design: "I will make a helper [the Hebrew is "helpmeet"] suitable for him" (2:18b NIV). Thus began the world's first partnership—a woman created to complement Adam's skills, while adding her own unique touch. The plan: to do more together than either one could do solo—an alliance of reliance.

Whether you do your work in solitary environments or participate in large teams or corporations, there are certain skill sets, gifts, or complements useful for you to thrive. What kind of people do you need to work with who can complement or bring out the best in you? Are those people already in your life? If not, recognize what you're looking for in a complementary person, company, or situation.

It's been said that when the student is ready, the teacher will arise. When you're ready, your complement may arise. It's time to be ready!

This chapter marks a crossroad for you, a time to decide, to discern: go, no, or slow? Reality can be a tough pill to swallow and a challenge to embrace. So we decided to end Part One of the book with our own heartfelt prayer for you.

Now as you embrace your true calling, accepting its privileges and its great responsibilities, may you willingly hold in tension your prior commitments, accepting them as God's best plan for your life. May you know when to move ahead with full steam and complete focus. May you also know when to stand still and listen. And by doing so, may you experience the thrill of living a life worthy of your calling—your life. Nothing more, nothing less, nothing else.

Actions Required

Fill out the action plan in Table 7.1 to help you discern actions that you must take before you can shift into higher gear and start moving toward living your career calling. Some of these actions might include finishing one more chapter in this book, consulting with a trusted adviser, or even just taking the time you need to reflect.

We have listed a place for you to select an accountability person who can help to guide you, consult with you, or more importantly hold you accountable. This person is someone who is in your corner and is aware of your search for your calling.

If you feel like you're not living your career calling, now is the time to start.

TABLE 7.1   Career Calling Action Plan

Task or Situation	Action Required	Projected Date Finished	Accountability Person

Finding the Job That Fits Your Calling

CHAPTER 8

The Résumé: Market Yourself with Words

YOU'RE IN COMPETITION with millions. Believe it or not, one online job posting can solicit thousands of résumés. From the highly qualified to the "Well, I might as well just give it a shot," there's no shortage of résumés. It's no different for ads posted in major newspapers. The company mailroom quickly swells with piles of résumés and cover letters for a single job.

One posting I (Tom) created in Los Angeles for a sales representative position drew a response of 450 résumés over the first weekend. It just about locked up my whole computer! In another instance my good friend Fred sent his résumé to a company and soon learned he was one of 650 candidates. Some tough odds, right? Though very capable and qualified for that position, Fred didn't get the job. He didn't even get a phone call or personal reply.

> ## Chapter Take-Aways
> - Learn how to create résumés that speak the reader's language.
> - Understand what type of résumé would best articulate your background.
> - Know how to create and sell yourself with follow-up materials.

Let's face it, the overwhelming majority of résumés are pretty much the same. They're usually documents neatly printed on $8\frac{1}{2}$-by-11-inch sheets of paper. Though vital to the job search process, the typical résumé can lull even the most caffeinated reader to sleep.

This doesn't mean that a résumé isn't a valuable tool. According to Webster's dictionary, a résumé "sums up a job applicant's qualifications and experience." Résumés communicate valuable information to hiring managers, so you need to ask yourself this all-important question: What can I do to make my résumé stand out?

Here are three principles you can use to better market yourself through your résumé.

Know Thy Audience

Expert communicators do one thing that separates them from the amateurs: they keep their audience in mind. They seek to understand before making others understand. It doesn't matter how loudly you speak and how clearly you enunciate if you're speaking English to someone who speaks only French. Recall the classic scene from the Peter Sellers movie *The Return of the Pink Panther*. Inspector Clouseau approaches a man who is standing next to a large dog. The French inspector reaches down to pat the dog on the head. He asks the man, "Sir, does your dog bite?" "No," he answers. With a sudden snap, the dog lunges and rips into Clouseau's hand. Clouseau shrieks in pain, "Sir, I thought you said your dog doesn't bite!" The gentleman replies, "That is not my dog."[1]

Like Clouseau, you possess the scars from a bitten hand or two. Maybe you wasted time by failing to start with the right questions. You can't afford to throw a résumé together in a rush. It expresses who you are and what you do best, and it tells the reader how you can add value to the organization.

Questions to ask yourself may include: Who should this speak to? What are these people like? What language do they speak? What jargon do they use? What format communicates professionalism and demonstrates an understanding of their world and relates it to my own? You may find answers to these questions by looking at the company's Web site. Or you may take a trip to the library and seek articles or books that include information on the company, its officers, policies, and vision. Ultimately, the best way to gain insight is to ask a current or former employee.

Be creative to stand apart from the crowd, but don't forget protocol.

In some instances your résumé-reading audience may not even be a person. More and more large companies use scanning programs that search through hundreds of résumés for key words. Human resource departments use this technology to streamline their candidate-screening process. They don't care whether you were captain of your college swim team or once started your own printing service. They scan for the technical or industry-oriented words they're looking for.

With this audience in mind, are there any key words you should consider placing somewhere in your résumé? The point is to get over the hurdle of the computerized reader and on to the human reader, your most important audience. What will that person be looking for?

- The basic format and style of your résumé.
- The different job titles you've had that may or may not represent skills transferable to the job you're applying for.
- Your education: where and what you studied, what level you achieved, whether you received any recognition or honors.
- The length of your résumé. Rule of thumb: résumés should rarely be more than two pages. In most industries less is more.
- The basic aesthetics and feel of the résumé: fonts, blank space, and choice of paper reflect who you are. And neatness counts.

Even the two of us look for different things in a résumé. Tom tends to take the spreadsheet approach: just the facts, please. "Bullets. Please give me bullets!" Jeff actually reads the words in the paragraphs and appreciates word choice and sentences that make sense. But we agree that a concise writing style, correct spelling, and a visually appealing presentation get the edge. A résumé isn't a novel or a complete list of every responsibility or accolade you've had since you were ten. It's an overview.

The simple truth is that not all résumé readers are the same. Here are five different types (or caricatures) you may encounter. As you read these extreme examples, realize that the people who read your résumé may be like one (or a combination) of these crazy characters.

The Five Types of Résumé Readers

The Gut Feeler

The gut feeler doesn't care about your résumé's logic or flow or even its syntax and grammar. He just gets a feeling about you, maybe because you're from New Jersey, just like him. "Who are you, and when can I see you here?"

The Perfectionist

The perfectionist is just the opposite. Grammar, spelling, syntax, font, paper quality—it *all* matters to the perfectionist. As she reviews your résumé, she notes that you misspelled *clerical* as *klerical* and uses her red marker to circle your misuse of commas. Then she separates the résumés into neat piles that she secures safely under paperweights.

The Paper Factory

There's more paper in this reviewer's office than in a Hallmark card factory. It will be a minor miracle if he'll even be able to find your résumé, let alone see it as urgent enough to give it a real read. You'll probably need to give the paper factory a follow-up call just to remind him your résumé even exists.

The Professional Staff

What the paper factory needs, the professional staff has: people power. Five other people will wade through the work the manager won't get to. Once your résumé enters their domain, staff will neatly track it as it works its way through the organized system of review and commentary.

The People Pleaser

The people pleaser places all the résumés into the "Call for interview" pile after review. The assistant then dutifully schedules interviews with each and every job applicant. People pleasers never want to make anyone feel bad.

Sometimes we come across individuals exactly like these five résumé-reading caricatures. You may meet someone who blends a couple of types. But as you figure out their type and get to know your audience, you become equipped to tailor your résumé to fit the needs of the recruiter or hiring manager.

Here are some questions to ask yourself about your audience:

How busy is their schedule?

How many résumés will they be receiving?

What are their standards for grammar, spelling, and punctuation?

What is their corporate or organizational culture—professional, trained, experienced, flexible, proficient, socially adaptable, creative?

Do they have an urgent need to fill a position, or will your résumé just be for browsing?

What are their professional values?

What words and skills would make me stand out in their mind?

Speak Their Language

We all size people up quickly based on their language. Even if we all speak English, we can quickly identify where in the country the other person comes from. Sometimes it's simply their greeting: "Howdy, y'all!" or "Hey, youse guys!" or "Gooood ahffftanoon." In fact, newscasters work hard at speaking a dialect that connects most broadly across many lines. Rarely will you catch a major network anchor saying, "It ain't gonna rain much tomorrah" or "It's gonna be fawty degrees outside when you pak yah cahh."

Résumés also convey a language. Recruiters say that they take approximately fifteen seconds to read a résumé to see if the applicant is qualified. (And most recruiters are not speed readers!)

Most people, whether hiring managers or recruiters, look deeper than just job titles, positions, time spent in roles, or level of education. They want to know if you have the ability to deliver a return on their investment in you. You will be taking a risk on them, and they will also be taking a risk on you.

Here are some basic tips:

If you're applying for a sales position, show your sales results with dollar signs and percentages of attainment.

If you're applying for a financial or accounting position, describe more of your training and how much money you've managed or saved the company in the past.

If you're working with software, list and describe the programs you've worked with and the programming languages you're proficient in.

If you're applying for a manufacturing job, list certifications that you have attained, such as forklift driver, or specific machines you've operated.

Industries and companies have certain words or phrases that let the reader know you're an insider, that you get it. A good way to become familiar with some of these terms is to visit industry or company Web sites or study their printed material. Notice what's important to them by looking at the words they choose. Read the company's mission statement and see whether and how much it matches your own passions, interests, or desires.

Of course, no one's going to create a different résumé for each company or interview, but you may be able to make some subtle but meaningful changes by taking note of key words, phrases, and values.

Choose the Appropriate Type of Résumé

A résumé sends a cultural message to people. There are a billion ways to create one. So where do you start?

We will discuss three basic types of résumés. Each of these is similar and yet different in the main message and the way it delivers information to the reader.

Keep in mind there are many great résumé books at your local bookstore or library and the professional services that specialize in writing résumés. Don't hesitate to ask for help. Hiring someone from a professional résumé service may well be worth your investment due to the impact this document can make. The two most notable certifications to look for in a résumé writer or service are Certified Professional Résumé Writer (CPRW) and Professional Association of Résumé Writers (PARW). You may want to ask prospective résumé writers if they have attained these certifications.

Obviously, résumés vary in style and look. But the most common types fall into three basic categories: chronological, functional, and combination.

The Chronological Résumé

The chronological résumé is the most traditional and most common. It simply lists your work experience and education, starting with your present job and moving backward in time. See Exhibit 8.1 for a sample.

EXHIBIT 8.1   Chronological Résumé

William Jones
4400 Main St.
Houston, TX 77007
wjones@email.com
713 555 1000 Cell 281 555 1000

OBJECTIVE   Seeking a position that offers potential for career development and an opportunity for advancement.

EXPERIENCE   1/2001–Present   ABC Corporation   Houston, TX

Sales Representative

Manage my own territory of Pasadena, Deer Park, La Porte, Baytown, Seabrook, Kemah, Clear Lake, and other parts of Houston. Responsible for developing potential prospects, setting appointments, and originating new business sales while continuing to serve established client base for my territory. Ranked ninth nationally in sales volume for third quarter FY 2002. Received a performance-based raise for volume sold during the second quarter FY 2002. Achieved above 100 percent of my weekly average quota during my first fiscal year with ABC. Awarded a 50 percent bonus of sold-dollar volume for having achieved high sales numbers for the third quarter fiscal year.

1/1997–1/2001   ABC Corporation   Houston, TX

Sales Associate

Developed prospective business contacts and initiated sales for myself and other sales representatives in ABC's overall territory for the Houston location. This position is used as an associate training period in preparation for management of own territory. Promoted to Sales Representative after only two months as a Sales Associate (six months is the average length of time before promotions are normally considered).

11/1993–1/1997   Winston's Office Equipment   Houston, TX

Sales Representative

Responsible for building and closing client base through marketing by appointments and cold calling. Prepared sales presentations using PowerPoint. Prepared document and productivity analysis for prospective clients. Promoted to Religious Vertical Market Representative in March 1996. Ranked number two Religious Market Representative overall in the U.S. for the year 1996. Ranked number one Religious Market Representative in the U.S. third and fourth quarter of 1996. Year 1996 sales total $205,000. Reached 100 percent of performance quota in first month of field activity and maintained and raised that percentage.

8/1991–8/1993   WM Management Company   Houston, TX

Leasing Agent

Showed and leased apartments to walk-in customers. Helped residents with problems that arose on a day-to-day basis.

EDUCATION   Boston University, MA
BA, Political Science

The chronological résumé does several things:

- Highlights your track record of accomplishment
- Lists your job title and time in the position
- Shows your growth in experience and responsibility
- Enables the reader to quickly assess what you've done and accomplished

The Functional Résumé

The functional résumé is organized around your skills, experiences, and accomplishments, not around your jobs. It focuses on your abilities and talents and lists your work experience in skill clusters (see Exhibit 8.2). It can be especially useful when you are considering a change in your career direction or if your employment record is spotty.

EXHIBIT 8.2 Functional Résumé

Betty Jones
24 Walker Ave., Barrington, IL 60010
Betjones@hotmail.com
(405) 555–9999

PROFILE

An energetic, self-motivated and hardworking Human Resources Coordinator with experience in all aspects of human resources. Able to use own initiative and work as part of a team. Proven leadership skills, including managing and motivating other staff to achieve company objectives. Good problem-solving and analytical skills. Computer literate.

HUMAN RESOURCE PLANNING

- Assessing the company's future staffing requirements over the short, medium, and long term

- Liaising with the company's senior management to determine their human resources requirements

- Producing a comprehensive human resources plan for the company's expansion over the next five years

RECRUITMENT & SELECTION

- Preparing and placing advertisements in the local and national press

- Interviewing candidates and checking references

- Producing job descriptions and contracts of employment

- Liaising with other departments in the company over candidate selection and rejection

- Coordinating with local high schools and universities

TRAINING & DEVELOPMENT

- Developing effective training programs in conjunction with other departments in the company

- Organizing and conducting induction training sessions for all new employees

- Appointing and monitoring external training organization for specialist training

EMPLOYEE SERVICES

- Managing and maintaining staff personnel records

- Counseling staff as and when required

- Organizing social activities as the Activities Officer of the staff social club
- Producing health and safety reports

EXPERIENCE

1/2000–Present	Human Resources Manager, ABC Company, Chicago, IL
11/1992–12/1999	Human Resources Coordinator, Blue Ribbon Manufacturing, Chicago, IL
1/1989–10/1992	Human Resources Clerk, Career Trainer Corporation, Barrington, IL

EDUCATION

Master of Labor and Human Resources, Oklahoma University, 2003

Bachelor of Science in Business Administration—Human Resources, Boston University, 1999

The functional résumé does the following things:

- Keeps the focus off past history if you have little or no experience and are seeking an entry-level job
- Emphasizes qualifications that might not be visible from a list of past titles or positions

The Combination Résumé

The combination résumé combines features from chronological and functional résumés. It combines your skills and accomplishments and clearly presents qualifications you have that might not be evident from past positions.

The combination résumé does the following:

- Highlights your transferable skills, accomplishments, and qualifications on one document.
- Makes a strong connection between your work experience and areas of responsibility. This helps the reader see how your skill sets can transfer to another situation.
- Highlights common strengths and abilities when your experience doesn't show a clear-cut career direction.

E-mail or Internet Résumé

You can also reach a hiring manager by posting a résumé on the Web or sending it by e-mail. The e-mail or Internet résumé can include elements of the other forms, but you must consider specific points when applying for a job electronically.

- Keep it simple: no fancy graphics, fonts, or formats. They may not transfer cleanly.

- Be careful in the use of vertical lines or bracketed information. They may not line up when printing.

- Set the page flush left. Centered text may print differently on the hiring manager's printer than on yours or may align differently on another reader's Internet browser.

- Don't use parentheses, underlining, and shading.

Consider adding extra key words to the end of your résumé—we mean a ton of key words! Why? Because scanning programs will pick up key words that may link your strengths, experiences, or accomplishments to their own search. These may be synonyms of other words already contained in the résumé or more technical words. List these at the bottom of the résumé, then change the font color to white. Although readers cannot see them with the naked eye, the human resources department's scanning program will pick them up and possibly move your résumé into the group for further review or even an interview. For more information on electronic résumés, see Chapter Ten.

Résumé Checklist

Before you send your résumé off to the printer or the hiring manager, put it through this checklist:

- ❑ The career objective is in line with the position that the employer posted.
- ❑ The body of the résumé supports my career objective.
- ❑ The résumé clearly answers the most important questions the employer will ask.
- ❑ The most important elements of my work experience appear on the top half of the first page.

- ❏ My résumé and especially my accomplishments begin with action verbs and are quantified when appropriate.
- ❏ The résumé uses present tense when talking about my current job and past tense when referring to past jobs.
- ❏ It's easy to read, to the point, with lots of white space.
- ❏ Someone else has proofread the résumé for grammar and typos.
- ❏ The résumé invites further interest.
- ❏ It projects an image I feel good about.
- ❏ It uses key words appropriate for the industry or the potential employer.
- ❏ It uses bold type, indentation, underlining, and bullets.

Cover Letters: To Use or Not to Use

You may or may not decide to create a cover letter for a personal introduction to your résumé and application. Writing a cover letter is part of the application process to some hiring managers, so let the manager decide whether they want to read it or not. Because I (Tom) like to get to the facts, I don't spend much time reading cover letters. But that's not to say that a cover letter is not an important document that you can include as a way to introduce yourself and your résumé. Some people consider it a valuable look at your personal style and a way to begin evaluating your abilities. A cover letter is a brief overview of who you are and why you are interested in the company or position. It's a first impression. It often relates the more personal information about you and can create a desire within the reader to read on.

Here are some things you may want to include in your cover letter:

An introduction of yourself.

An explanation of why you are contacting the manager.

A brief summary of the talents you possess and how they may align with the position.

A personalized message to the company you are sending it to. (Others can tell when they are reading a form letter. Can't you?)

Your letter should contain three paragraphs (and probably no more): (1) a brief introduction of who you are and why you are writing to them, (2) a description of what you bring to the table and how it can help them, and (3) a thank-you for taking the time to consider you as a candidate.

Additional Documents

In preparing your résumé, you will want to have some other documents and information in your tool kit. These include references and an executive summary.

References

Although you need not send out a list of references with your résumé, it's still important to know who will confirm your gifts, attributes, and accomplishments. These people provide a valuable commodity for you and for your potential employer: a verification of your qualifications.

This list of people can include past supervisors, peers, customers, vendors, and people who've known you for a long time. These people will be able to describe your strengths and character traits without hesitation. Before listing the three or more people, you will want to ask to make sure that they would feel comfortable doing this. If they don't, or if you don't feel confident that they will say positive things, then you will need to find someone else. The last thing you want is to be surprised by what a reference said during a reference check.

Print your reference list on an $8\frac{1}{2}$-by-11-inch piece of paper and include the following:

- Name of contact
- Contact's company or organization and current position (for example, president, controller)
- Relationship to you (supervisor, peer, and so on)
- Contact phone number(s)

Executive Summary

An executive summary is a way to highlight some of the key points you would like an interviewer to remember about you. You are taking the time to prepare the notes you would want them to take at an interview. Not all interviewers take great notes, and this is a way to reiterate who you are and indicate that you are the perfect hire. Even if you are not applying for a senior-level job, this kind of extra demonstrated effort and self-marketing can leave a lasting impression. Of course, you will want to use your judgment as to whether this suits your style or the type of position you seek. But it certainly is the kind of thing your competition (other applicants) may not be doing.

An effective way to use this tool is simply to give it to your interviewer after an interview and say, "I've prepared an executive summary for you. It describes some of what we spoke about today and what I can bring to this position."

An executive summary should be no more than one page and can include any of the following elements. The elements you include will vary depending on the type of position you are applying for.

- Key accomplishments
- Management experience
- Technical experience
- Awards and recognition
- Impacts that increased sales
- Impacts that decreased expenses
- Impacts that increased profits
- Training and education

Under each major heading, list two to four bullet points (with only one line per bullet). Try to keep it to four major headings with two to four minor bullet points under each one. Keep it brief. Remember that you are just hitting major points.

A Thank-You Note or Follow-Up Letter

A thank-you note may not seem like a big deal, but it really is! In it you express gratitude and let the reader know that you understand and appreciate that he or she invested time and energy with you. Rarely does anyone feel that a thank-you note is an imposition—just the opposite. They notice that you took the time and had the professional courtesy to follow up after your meeting.

How to Write a Résumé and Other Important Documents

Start with the basics, the fundamentals, the key elements.

Your Name and Vital Information

Your name should be bold and in a font larger than the rest (at least fourteen points). Give your complete address: include your home phone, cell, and work numbers. Give them as many numbers as possible. If one is busy or there's no answer, you want to offer the best shot to get your live voice on the other end of the line. When recruiters or hiring managers call, they would prefer to reach you immediately.

Give your e-mail address. If you don't have a computer, by all means use one at the library and sign up for an e-mail address that you can access wherever you are.

Summary or Objective

Set it out right up front. You may take either of two approaches here. Approach number one is to write a summary of what you want to do. The snapshot you want the reader to see here is of you in the best-case scenario at the company, doing what you're great at. It's the vision thing.

Approach number two is to provide a short description of what you have been trained to do. This sums up the past and brings it right to the present.

We recommend that you state in one sentence or very brief paragraph what you are capable and fully qualified to do. Based on the spadework you did in the first part of this book, this text uses active and energetic language to tell the reader, "This is what I do." "Almost can't help doing it!" "I can't not do this!"

Work Experience

This is the part that everyone looks at carefully: where you have worked, what you have done, and what you accomplished while doing it. List the most relevant jobs first.

If you are writing a résumé for the first time, here are the basics.

Company Name, City, State, Dates in Position

Your job title. Set this in a bold font. You want the reader to immediately notice titles and recognize companies.

Responsibilities and duties. Include relevant experience that identifies the key responsibilities and duties that you had in each position that you held. Describe what you did and what your tasks were, either in a bulleted list or one or two sentences. If this is your most recent job, you will want this to be the most complete look at what you can and have done.

Accomplishments or achievements. Focus on what you yourself accomplished or achieved. When putting this part of your résumé together, think of questions like these: What awards and recognition did I receive? What impact did I make that helped the company or department I worked in? If you don't have key accomplishments to list (due to the nature of your work), just beef up your responsibilities and duties.

Education

Degree. Write, for example, "BA in Business Administration" or "High School Diploma."

School name and location. Keep in mind that alumni typically like other alumni from the same school. Or perhaps the hiring manager was raised in the city where you went to college.

Date of degree. This is optional, with arguments on both sides on this issue. If you are at the beginning of your career or more than 50 years old, you really date yourself; however, some employers really like to see the dates to make sure you indeed have a completed degree. We tend to leave the date off, but what you do is up to you.

Special Training or Certifications

Training classes. If you are in sales, this is a great spot to briefly list some of the training classes you've taken. If you took the class in the last two years, list the date; if you took it twenty years ago, you may want to leave the date off.

Certifications. If you are the information technology field, you are aware of how important certifications can be. This can also be true for other fields as well, so if you have any that apply to the position you're seeking, list them.

CHAPTER 9

Create Your Action Room

MILITARY LEADERS call it the situation room; others call it command central, op center, or the war room. We call it an action room. When national security is threatened, leaders assemble in one location to centralize information, communication, and strategic planning. At critical times the action room becomes the nexus and the nerve center to study, decide, and execute action when important things are at stake.

When it's time to find the job that fits your calling, one of the most important first steps is to create your own version of the action room. Choose a space and prepare it for action.

I (Tom) learned the value of this critical step the hard way. In my past job searches, I made the mistake of using what I call Post-it-note organization. I sprinkled notes, numbers, and follow-up reminders throughout the bedroom, living room, and—the biggest mistake—the kitchen. With two teenagers and the regular rush hour traffic of a busy family, my notes were in constant danger of having syrup and coffee spilled on them or of being tossed into the trash. Everything was scattered and in disorder. I felt stressed and frustrated, but I was the only one to blame. Don't let this happen to you! Get organized.

Creating your action room involves designating a space where you won't be in danger of misplacing valuable contact information or notes pertaining to your search. It means setting aside one physical location to create a focused and strategic

> ### *Chapter Take-Aways*
> - Learn how to set up an action room.
> - Gain the tangible materials to function most effectively.
> - Map a strategy for moving from ideas to implementation.

approach. One of the most valuable things I teach people in seminars is simply to make the commitment to arrange and set aside a place as their personal command center.

How to Make Your Action Room

Setting up an action room requires only a few steps.

Create a Sign of Your Commitment

Should you decide to accept this mission (imagine the *Mission Impossible* theme song playing in the background), failure is not an option. Distractions, rejections, and the stuff of everyday life will get in the way of your goal. But as the saying goes, every great journey begins with a single step. Challenge yourself by asking: Where do I want to be one year from today?

Where will I be? _____

Doing what? _____

Accomplishing what? _____

Are you willing to make a commitment? If so, what do you plan to change?

My Commitments

❑ I am not going to fall back into a routine of haphazardly searching through newspapers or countless job boards. I will have a plan.

❑ I will not accept just any type of job.

❑ I will devote _____ hours a week in this primary pursuit.

❑ I will find the job that fits my talents.

It is important to represent your goal of finding the job that fits your calling in some tangible way. Writing it down can help. Fill in your name and the date in the blanks provided in Exhibit 9.1.

EXHIBIT 9.1   My Contract

I, ———————————, commit to create an action room by ———————
and will not look back once I do. I will not fail in finding the job that fits my calling, so help
me God.

Pick a Definite Space

This should be a location in your home that's private and quiet, ideally a room with
a door. The key here is to establish an environment where you can work and stay
focused during phone calls and search activities. You may be limited in your space
selection, and you may have to use a computer where the kids work too. If space is
limited, you may even need to create a mobile office that you can set up and take
down. Or head for the dining room table if it's not used frequently.

   The point here is that you want the action room to serve you and help you stay
focused on your mission in your mind and in your actions.

   What room or space will you choose?

Equip the Room

Purchase or find the following supplies:

- Two pads of paper
- Highlighters (in three colors)
- Pens
- Map of your local area
- Pushpins
- A piece of tag board or foam board
- File folders
- A compass
- A place to store files

Set Up an Area Map

If you were to visit your local fire station, you would almost certainly find an area
map on the wall. It hangs in a prominent spot and contains the detailed depiction of
districts that each firefighter should know inside and out. Firefighters have learned

that having defined districts and boundaries helps them be efficient in fighting fires and meeting their community's needs.

Use a map to help you define the geographical area of your search. Commuting may be a positive thing for you, or it may be nasty, brutish, and long! The commute is an important aspect of the job search that is easy to overlook. If you prefer trains to traffic, you may want to include a map of area commuter lines. Stay focused on workplaces that fall within your chosen area.

Practical Steps

1. Attach a local, regional, or metro area map to a bulletin or foam board.

2. Hang the map in your action room.

3. Put a pushpin in your home location on the map.

4. Use a compass to establish your commuting range.

Draw a circle that would establish your thirty-minute commute from home, identified as zone one (see Figure 9.1). Then do this again to establish a sixty-minute commute, zone two. If you don't mind traveling by car or train, draw a ninety-minute range.

FIGURE 9.1   My Commute Range

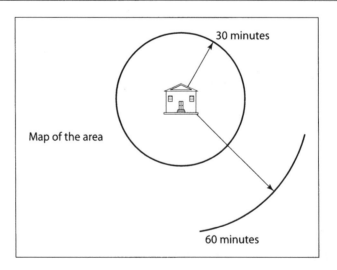

Set Up Tracking Files

You will want to record the contacts you make and résumés you send out. When the phone rings, you need instant access to information and reminders of the person you've spoken to, the position, and the location. Nothing's more frustrating to a recruiter or hiring manager than calling a prospective employee and hearing that the person doesn't remember who they are or what job they applied for. It just doesn't look very professional.

Here are some of the things you need to track:

- Networking contacts
- Direct contacts (see Chapter Twelve)
- Résumés
- Passwords for job boards and Internet access
- News articles and ads
- Job searching expenses

Use Table 9.1 as a form to record the résumés you send out on the Internet and in response to job ads.

Planning ahead will save you time and trouble. The idea here is to create a space both physically and emotionally to go out and find the job you love. By doing this now, you will streamline your search and prepare your mind for action. Do yourself a favor and stay organized.

TABLE 9.1   Tracking Internet and Job Ads

Date Applied	Company Name	Web Site	City Location	Zone 1 or 2	Position Title	Contact Name	Job Board or Ad	Sent Résumé	Follow-up Date 1	Follow-up Date 2

CHAPTER 10

Doing Your Homework

Using the Library and the Web

T HE SHOW is about to start. The audience packs the auditorium, and the anticipation builds because the curtain will soon go up. The actors and actresses are dressed and prepared. They're all counting on you, for tonight is *your* night. You're playing the lead role.

But there's only one problem: you're not ready! You know you have lines, but you failed to study them. You're supposed to wear a costume, but it's nowhere to be found. As the curtain ascends, you start to feel your chest tighten and your palms sweat.

What do you need to know to be ready? Sometimes we just don't know what we don't know. Like the actor preparing for a role, everything that goes on behind the scenes and before showtime will help you to get ready. Your job is to do the following:

- Find out what you don't know.
- Know where to go to find that information.
- Organize what you learn.
- Use what you learn.

> ### Chapter Take-Aways
>
> - Learn how to use the library and reference librarian in your career search.
> - Discover new sources that can assist you in your search for information.
> - Create a list of businesses or companies to target in your job search.

When you consider the time, energy, and effort that you'll need to find the job of your calling, doesn't it makes sense to do some work in advance? You've taken the time to define who you are and what you're called to. You know your values, your strengths, and your gifts. Now it's time to shift gear and get into information-gathering mode. What's out there that fits your gifts? Who can help you learn more about resources?

The good news is that a lot of easily accessible information is out there. Now we're going to show you how to find it. Ready, get set, go!

Learn What's Out There

Today you can find data on companies and job opportunities quickly and easily. With increased technology and access to books and reference information, you can drill much deeper than ever before. Company history, the CEO's vision, the financial data, and even managers' names and biographies are easily available. Information that might have taken many hours or months to gather in the past can now be available in a matter of seconds.

The two primary places to access information are the library and the Internet. Though it may be easy to think that the Web approach has surpassed the library, both provide you with valuable tools and resources. Here is a simple comparison:

What's Out There	*Library*	*Web*
Sources to help in your career search	Many	Many
How information is organized	Periodicals, books, reference tools	Web sites
Subsections of organization	Individual book or source	Links
New information vehicles	New books (like this one)	New Web sites
Places to meet people	Tables, rooms	Chat rooms and e-mail forums

What's Out There	Library	Web
Speed of information	Usually slower	Faster unless you lock up or crash
Point of inquiry	Reference librarian	Search engines
Community network events	Offered periodically	Chat rooms
Career-training programs	Programs designed for job seekers	How-to Web sites or online learning
Past articles and information	Articles within the database on companies and hiring managers	Some info available but tough to find
Access to computers and printers	Usually no charge	Can be costly

Start with the Library

The library's tools give you access to expert researchers and information. It may even serve as a temporary office and get you away from home or your present work environment. You may even meet someone in the library or parking lot who is also there as a potential employer to find sources for people to fill positions. (You can rest assured that that same person won't randomly knock on your front door that day.) A library can serve as another place to network.

The Reference Librarian

Let's just admit it: we've spent way too much time in a library trying to find something by ourselves, when sitting right in the middle of the reference section is a trained research expert whose job and mission is to help us find information. Reference librarians have been schooled in storing, finding, and using data to meet the needs of information seekers. In fact, most libraries require that reference librarians have earned a master's degree in library science.

Though they've been stereotyped as stern, unapproachable, and introverted, these people are happiest when they help you find what you're looking for. Of course, you may think of the librarian of your youth who nagged you to please be quiet and taught you the Dewey decimal system as one of the most important things in life. OK, so they were wrong on that! But at this juncture, they may be the most valuable player of your career search.

Here's what you do: after putting your stuff down, head directly to the reference desk. Introduce yourself: "Hi, my name is. . . . I'm here to find information on. . . . Do you have anything that you think can help, and can you direct me to it? Or do you have any suggestions?"

You'll find that some of the most valuable sources for a search are located directly behind the reference librarian's desk. The librarian can introduce you to new reference sources such as a new periodical or computer software program. In addition, some of the more expensive sources may not even be accessible without the librarian's assistance.

The key here is to ask for help. Don't worry about needing the library-for-dummies approach on this.

Tips for Working with the Reference Librarian

We went directly to the experts and gained these tips:

- You may want to call to make an appointment. This enables the librarian to find information and prepare for a one-on-one meeting.
- Briefly explain the nature of your search and what you hope to accomplish.
- Ask what sources are the most valuable.
- If you're unsure about a source, ask how to use it or how it works.
- Ask about other locations outside the library where you might find this kind of information. ("Is there anyone else I should speak with?")
- Thank them. (They are a valuable part of your team.)

As one head reference librarian said, "The Internet is fine, but it doesn't reason through your needs like a reference librarian can."

Some Library Sources

Though there are ever-changing updates, new editions, and new sources, you may use the old reliables in Figure 10.1 as a starting point.

FIGURE 10.1   Some Library Sources

Source: *Manufacturers Guide*
Where to find it: At reference librarian's desk.
What it is: This list of manufacturing companies is
broken down by city and gives key information about each company.
How to use it: Search by city, looking for companies
that fit your location, size, and type.

Source: *Service Directory*
Where to find it: At reference librarian's desk.
What it is: This lists companies that provide a service
or are in service industries. It also lists
pertinent information on each company
and is broken down by city.
How to use it: Search by city, looking for companies
that fit your location, size, and type.

Source: *Chamber of Commerce Directory*
Where to find it: At reference librarian's desk.
What it is: This directory lists companies that belong
to a city's chamber of commerce.
How to use it: You can review companies by name or
by company type.

Source: *Dun & Bradstreet*
Where to find it: Reference section.
What it is: This lists companies' financial situation
and ratings.
How to use it: Research companies' key officers and
financial ratings investigate their ability
to manage flow of money and capital.

Source: *Thomas Register*
Where to find it: Reference section.
What it is: This directory gives a breakdown of
companies by industry or service type.
How to use it: Use this to find the locations of
companies and organizations in the
industry sector you have selected.

(*Continued*)

FIGURE 10.1   Some Library Sources (*Continued*)

Other Sources for Company Information
D&B Million Dollar Directory
Directory of Corporate Affiliations
S&P Corporations
Encyclopedia of Associations
Encyclopedia of Business Information

Other Sources for Information About Occupations
Encyclopedia of Careers and Vocational Guidance
Occupational Outlook Handbook
American Almanac of Jobs & Salaries

One of the sources listed in Figure 10.1, the *Occupational Outlook Handbook*, may serve as a starting point to uncover or evaluate occupations worth considering. This tool can help you pinpoint jobs that closely align with your calling and abilities. It provides the following information:

Nature of the work. What is this job like?

Working conditions. What is its location and environment?

Employment opportunities. What are the statistics within this occupation?

Training and qualifications. What's required for this job?

Job outlook. What does the future hold for this occupation?

Earnings. What range of income can you expect?

The Web

Of course, the Internet is the other source of amazing facts, opportunities, and marketing. There are many ways to use this technological tool. Here are three of the more common for your job search:

- Researching what and who is out there
- Posting your résumé
- Applying for a job

Internet Research

Approach your Internet research as a modern way to arm yourself with the data to pinpoint and connect your calling with an opportunity. The Internet provides you with a front-row seat to understand

- Company mission statements
- Basic company history
- Description of products and services
- Job openings
- Key company officers and their background
- Company location and environment
- Key competitors and industry information

Thousands, maybe millions of sites and links provide ways to fully research companies, trends, and opportunities. We hesitate to list too many Web sites because they may be obsolete and replaced by new ones by the time you read this. You can find the Web sites either by searching through major search engines or asking your reference librarian. The bookstore and library also contain books on the latest Internet sites and career sources.

Here are a few long-running sites:

Hoovers.com (http://hoovers.com): Information on companies and their competitors with some financial stats companies

Business.com (http://business.com): Information and links to thousands of U.S. companies

EDGAR (http://www.sec.gov/edgarhp.htm): Analysis and information that companies have filed with the U.S. Securities and Exchange Commission

Posting Your Résumé

The Internet is a great tool for search information, but it also provides a direct link for marketing yourself through the posting of your résumé. Though you shouldn't rely too much on this venue, it is a way to get more exposure.

There are a couple of things you want to be careful about with this approach. First of all, everyone will see your information, maybe even your current employer. (This may be unlikely, but it has happened and is certainly possible.) Even if you post your résumé as confidential (by removing your name and current company name), people who know you may still recognize you. Second, your résumé may remain on the Internet for years if you don't delete it. This can become a nuisance if you value privacy and are not interested in being contacted for every job that comes down the pike.

If you are going to post your résumé online, consider the following points:

Use the résumé you have already created in your word processing program, then cut and paste to fill in required information.

Avoid using boxes and lines in the document because these may not line up once posted.

Use confidential postings when seeking some degree of anonymity.

Keep a record of Web sites you've posted to in order to make further updates or deletions (see Table 9.1 for a tracking form).

Use the same or similar username and password for each Web site and keep track of them. Remember: keep it simple!

Be sure to create great punch lines or headers that will attract attention and may cause the viewer to open your résumé (for example: Master's Degree in Electrical Engineering with Fifteen Years' Experience).

Be sure to fill in all the information requested.

Create your own Web site and post your résumé and biography there. You can do this easily and inexpensively through major Web hosts.

Applying for Job Openings

Thousands of jobs are listed out there on the Web, and thousands of people are fighting for those same jobs. If you choose this way to find a career or calling, you need to understand that others out there may see this job not as their calling but more as a job that pays the bills. And they may have more experience than you.

Many people have found the Internet application a great way to land a job. This signals interest and can lead to follow-up discussions and possibly interviews. Of course, the reality is that most people who apply for a job online never hear back. But because you may be one of hundreds or thousands, you can do things to stand out and increase the possibility of getting an interview.

There are some things you can't change, like your background or experience. But some things can help you stand out from everyone else. We call these the three Ps:

Presentation: the way your document looks and feels to the reader.

Purpose: why you've sent this application and what you seek to bring to this opportunity.

Persistence: following up by phone or e-mail on a résumé or application demonstrates interest and desire.

Here are some points to consider when responding to online job listings:

Keep a record of the jobs you've applied for. Nothing's worse than when a recruiter or hiring manager calls and you don't remember even applying!

Locate important e-mail addresses through the company Web site or by calling the hiring department directly.

When possible, send a direct e-mail instead of applying through the job-board Web site. (This can set you apart because your message will go directly into an e-mail inbox.)

You may send a brief cover letter in the body of an e-mail and include your résumé as an attachment or paste it in the body of the e-mail as well. I usually suggest attachments, but some companies don't allow attachments from people outside the company, so pasting may be your only way in.

When possible, call the person you are applying to and stress your interest and purpose in sending the application or résumé. At that time you may even ask for an interview.

CHAPTER 11

Networking

Who Do I Know Who Can Help?

L IKE MANY GOOD THINGS, your network is already part of the fabric of your life. It's the common people, experiences, memories, and challenges that link you to others. It may be something you built intentionally over a long period or a list of people and experiences that is constantly changing. Companies can put a value on a candidate's network of contacts when considering that person for a job. Whom does this candidate influence? If they align with us, will their network of friends, associates, and connections align with us as well? Will they bring in new business or build our firm's credibility?

> ### Chapter Take-Aways
>
> - Identify different network categories and individuals to create pathways for your search.
> - Get information on individual contacts and develop an action plan to get in touch.
> - Don't be afraid to ask your network to help open a door or lead you to an opportunity.

In the best sense, your network is your association of trusted allies. Robin Hood had a band of merry men; King Arthur had his knights; the president has his cabinet. And you should strive to have your own inner core. Like circles that emanate from the impact of a stone thrown in a smooth pond, your network moves outward from the center. It moves from your deepest commitments to more casual acquaintances.

You know someone's in the inner ring when you can call them in the middle of the night if you are in a crisis. It wouldn't be awkward, and you know they wouldn't hesitate to help. You would do the same for them. These kinds of trusted connections may include your family and your most trusted friends. They may include a high school buddy, a sorority sister, or a former colleague. As you seek career change, don't hesitate to share with these people what you're looking for. Think about it: Wouldn't you help them if they made a similar request? "I'm searching for a job that fits my strengths. Do you know anyone I should talk to?"

Try to think about your sphere of influence. You might create a diagram like the one in Figure 11.1. The diagram will help you figure out all of your possible contacts. You may know more people than you think!

Sphere of Influence: Who's in Your Network?

This sphere of contacts and people to network with is just the start of this process. Hopefully this overview will get you to think how far your network reaches.

FIGURE 11.1   My Sphere of Influence

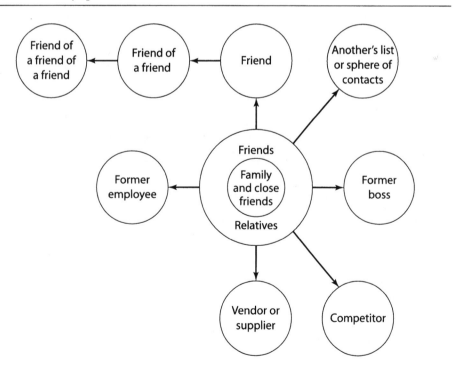

Cause a RUCKUS

Do you know what a ruckus is? Think back for a moment to your childhood. You and your little brother decided to have a friendly wrestling match in the living room. "Mom won't mind!" Before long, lamps were tumbling and noses bleeding. Your little brother screamed your name at record decibel levels, and Mom screamed even louder. That's a ruckus! A ruckus can be positive. It can be used to create attention and even momentum. If you've stumbled on street performers in a crowded downtown area, you probably were attracted to them because they knew how to create a ruckus. And you know what happens? Passersby get interested. They join in. They start cheering. And before long a small group becomes a large crowd of participants.

This is your chance to create your own network ruckus. Get your contacts working to help you fulfill your career calling.

Here are six steps for you to create effective ruckus networking. You'll notice they spell out the word *ruckus*. OK, bear with us. We're trying to create one too.

*R*elate casually.

*U*pdate them.

*C*ommunicate your calling.

*K*now your direction.

*U*nderstand their network.

*S*eek referrals.

Relate casually. Start with building rapport and focus on the relationship. Ultimately, relationships lead to more relationships and opportunities. Connect with your contacts. Care about what they care about. "Joe, I heard you guys had a new baby. That's great! A boy, huh? Wow, that makes four for you and Sarah! Congratulations."

Update them. Now it's your turn. When they ask, "How are you doing?" Tell them what's really going on. Share your current situation. "Kelly, I don't know if you heard what I'm up to these days. I've actually been downsized from my last position and am looking for a new opportunity. I have recently completed a process that helped me discover my career strengths and possibly even my calling. Can I share with you what I've learned and get your feedback?"

Communicate your calling. This may require you to discuss what you mean by *calling*. Share your passion and your desire to use your gifts in your work. In a nutshell, tell them what you do best. "I've worked in a few different positions. But honestly, I really feel my calling is to play a creative role through advertising. I want to use my gifts and passion to help small-business owners get their message out."

Know your direction. This is the chance to talk with some who can directly or indirectly get you pointed in the right direction within your chosen field. "I've heard that the advertising industry is booming here in Chicago. What I'm really looking for is a group of people who think out of the box to hook up with."

Understand their network. They know people that you don't. Some of those people can open doors for you. Find out what kind of people they know. "John, I realize you know some influential business people in the city—particularly in the pharmaceutical field. As I considered my approach to this career move, I thought of you and was wondering if you might be able to direct me or put me in touch with someone."

Seek referrals. Be direct here. Ask for names, numbers, and e-mail addresses of people who might help you directly or indirectly. "Would you be able to put me in contact with anyone from that downtown group that would have knowledge directly or indirectly related to what I'm looking for?"

If the network contact is someone you already know, you may need to spend more time talking with him or her than you would with someone you have never met. If the contact person is someone you've never met, start by finding common ground.

Who do you know in common? If someone referred you, mention that person.

What interests or involvements do you share?

What common experiences have you had?

What's important to them (a hobby or other interest)? Ask about it.

After you call, you'll need to take two important actions. First, update your database and networking worksheet (Worksheet 11.1). Second, send a thank-you note. In a world that's gotten used to e-contact, a handwritten note is a point of contact that will stand out from the crowd. Most people appreciate the personal touch of a handwritten note and will open those letters first when they get their mail.

Name: _____

Home address: _____

_____

Home e-mail: _____

Relationship: _____

Position: _____

Company/business: _____

Company address: _____

_____

Type of industry or business: _____

Business e-mail: _____

Office phone: _____

Cell phone: _____

Home phone: _____

Best time to catch them: _____

People They Have Referred Me To

Name: _____

Relationship: _____

Name: _____

Relationship: _____

Name: _____

Relationship: _____

History

Date of last contact: _____

Topic of last contact: _____

_____

Follow-up needed: _____

Date of last contact: _____

Topic of last contact: _____

_____

Follow-up needed: _____

Date of last contact: _____

Topic of last contact: _____

_____

Follow-up needed: _____

Superconnectors

It's amazing how many people most of us really know. We're all connected in some way, but some people are more connected than others. Those are the people that really tend to work at it, like our friend Bob. We call him and others like him superconnectors. For example, Bob, an executive recruiter, has a extensive base of contacts all over the country. Just call Bob with a question, and he can link you to someone in Dallas, Boise, or Boston. Such master networkers maintain Rolodexes and Palm Pilots filled to capacity. Others possess a more intimate network. They know fewer people, but they know them really well. But everybody knows somebody. Everybody's life touches the lives of others. And much of what takes place in business, politics, religion, or sales happens through networks, whether at the health club aerobics class, the scrapbooking club, or the soccer game. This is where people make deals and share information. Shift into higher gear and put these networkers to work.

Now we want to give you a few networking tips. Consider or check the ones you believe to be most vital for you now.

Networking Tips

- ❑ See everyone you meet as a potential link in a chain of influence—even the waiter at your favorite restaurant!
- ❑ Before you make the call, do your homework on what you hope to gain and on the common ground you may share.
- ❑ Give a referral and you may get one in return.
- ❑ Keep sowing seeds. Networking can be a numbers game. You never know what's going to pan out.
- ❑ Join an association or a networking group (for example, executive groups or chamber of commerce).
- ❑ Networking starts in no special place. Stop by and just introduce yourself.
- ❑ Set a time and a contact goal for yourself daily or weekly.
- ❑ Get organized and keep track of who you have talked with and other vital information. Use any forms, software, or even just a piece of paper if that works for you.
- ❑ If you run into a dry spell, keep at it!

Relationship Categories

It's possible that you underestimate the sheer scope and power of your current network. You may never have taken the time to really compile a list of all the people you are linked with. Consider some of these groupings:

- Childhood friends
- High school teammates
- College or grad school professors or classmates
- People who belong to the same church or service organization
- Neighbors, friends, and relatives
- Former bosses, employees, or coworkers
- Competitors who work in your industry
- Vendors or suppliers
- Teachers or trainers from classes you attended
- Clubs you belong to
- People with whom you share a hobby
- Your accountant
- Your doctor
- Your spiritual leader
- Your financial adviser
- Your recruiter

Harvey Mackay wrote in his book on networking, *Dig Your Well Before You're Thirsty,* "If I had to name the single characteristic shared by all the truly successful people I've met over a lifetime, I'd say it's the ability to create and nurture a network of contacts."[1] This is a lifelong process that should never stop because your network helps you in your everyday life. It opens doors and keeps them open.

Grab a few sheets of paper or use the format we provide in Table 11.1 and start brainstorming. We would suggest listing at least two hundred people. You'll be amazed at who comes to mind or who you find in old Christmas and holiday card lists.

TABLE 11.1   Networking List

Name	Relationship	Location	Phone	Action

Don't be afraid to use your network at all times in your career. Use this chapter's worksheet and table to keep track of your contacts. Remember that most people change jobs at least seven times or move three to five times during a career, so you'll need to keep updating and organizing these forms.

CHAPTER 12

Taking It to the Streets

IN A DECADE usually characterized more by lethargy than liveliness, the 1970s band the Doobie Brothers released a song titled "Taking It to the Streets." Today the song is far from a distant relic of rock memorabilia. A recent political campaign chose this as its theme song. Sound speakers blared the lyrics as the impassioned candidate arrived at an auditorium packed with voters.

In this chapter we want to encourage you to follow that anthem: take it to the streets. It's time to enlist the support of others who can help you take your next step. In the previous chapters, you discovered that you have been created and equipped for your life's calling. Now it's time to move into the mainstream and market your message and abilities. Let go of the status quo and start taking action.

> ## Chapter Take-Aways
>
> - Be able to articulate your value in a clear and concise statement.
> - Know how to discover jobs that others didn't know existed.
> - Develop a targeted list of companies or organizations you want to pursue.

Many people who possess unmistakable gifts still consider themselves unworthy of jobs in which they could put those gifts into practice. They think others won't want what they have to offer. You may feel that if it were meant to be, the phone would ring, the "you've got mail" voice would summon you, or an angel would appear bearing a telegram: "Behold, you have been chosen to be vice president of the ACME Widget Company. Follow me and enter into thy life work."

But you may still feel that you're imposing on a person when you seek out their help. Let us ask you this: Might your asking be the gift that enables someone else to do what they do best? Could your talent be just what causes an organization to move into its own higher gear?

Recently a Chicago businessman shared with me (Jeff) his experience with a twenty-seven-year-old pastor thirty years ago. "This young pastor asks if he can take a look at our new office headquarters," he said. "Honestly, I thought, *is this guy for real?* He looked more like a fraternity guy than a pastor. After I took him around the place, the pastor tells me, 'My church wants to purchase land and build a facility a lot like this one.' I was stunned," the businessman told me. "Does he have any idea what something like this cost? Is his head in the clouds or what? Yet sure enough, thirty years later, I get stuck in traffic when I drive by that enormous church. I give the guy credit: he knew what he wanted, and he went after it!"

Dominoes start to fall when you make the first move. You start making call after call, sharing your message and inviting others, and things happen. Finding a job is a contact sport, and you will need to make contacts. Don't sit by the phone waiting, hoping, and praying for an opportunity. Finding the job that fits requires your chutzpah and your willingness to hunt.

What You'll Need

When we consider seeking out the work we want, we tend to focus on tools such as résumés, endorsements, and a leather binder. Those are important, but those are just the externals, the icing on the cake.

The most vital equipment you'll need as you take it to the streets is the internal equipment. What you need most comes from within you.

But that doesn't mean you can't (or shouldn't) prepare. If you are preparing to take your calling to the streets and find a position, you can't afford to do so without the following four things:

- Positive mental outlook
- Product knowledge
- Action plan
- Knowledge of the hidden job market

Positive Mental Outlook

Some people seem to be born happy. They don't sweat the small stuff, and it all seems to be small stuff. Then they write books on how to be happy, and the rest of us wonder why their method doesn't work for us. Most of us feel disgruntled and have mood swings from time to time.

We experience our share of negative thoughts, down days, and blue moods. We fall off mountaintops and hit rock bottom, but we bounce back. "OK, so that time, I put my foot in my mouth and acted like a fool." But we get back up and move forward anyway.

Although thinking about what's gone wrong and what stinks may be a form of honesty, we can suck the life out of ourselves and those closest to us over time if we only stew and ruminate about those things. Misery loves company and has a way of pulling others into its unhappy vortex. If you're experiencing a time of uncertainty: don't do it! Don't let negative thoughts take root in you or in your household. Clean them out right away.

The alternative is to create an internal environment of positive mental outlook by promptly noticing the negative thoughts seeping in. Acknowledge them, but then insert positive ones or a reminder of your resolve in their place. If inserting positive thoughts feels dishonest, at least do something else with your mind: pray, go for a walk, read something positive, work out. Paul writes, "Whatever is pure, whatever is noble, whatever is right, whatever is lovely, whatever is admirable—if anything is excellent or praiseworthy . . . think about such things" (Philippians 4:9 NIV).

As you hit the streets, maintain a positive mental outlook.

Product Knowledge

You will also need to be prepared with the knowledge of your product: your skills and talents, what you do best. Use this to prepare what sales trainers call the elevator speech. Consultants call it the mission or purpose statement. It's a statement of who you are and what you do in a nutshell.

How do you take your expansive product knowledge and make it simple enough for those willing to hear what you have to say? It may come down to answering the casual question: "So what do you do?" Or it may come up in an interview: "OK, so what can you do for me?" Without pulling out a résumé with a litany of degrees and past positions or fumbling with vague statements like "I'm a consultant" or "I'm a salesperson," what do you do? Like Buddy in the 1980s movie *Wall Street*, day after day of cold calling can come down to the moment when the prospect finally gives you some time and attention. Nervously sitting in the prestigious office of Gordon Gecko, Buddy gets his chance. Gecko eyeballs Buddy and asks him, "OK, Kemo Sabe, why am I listening to you?" It's exactly what Buddy's been seeking day after day, but he's not prepared. He stutters and bumbles, then blurts out dangerous insider information he hadn't intended to share.[1]

What will you say when they say "yes," when they meet with you, when they bring you in to speak with the president? What will you say when they ask, "Why am I listening to you?" When you can articulate your product knowledge (what you do) in one compelling sentence and feel good about it, you're probably ready to answer that question.

Here are some examples: "I maximize the effectiveness of task-oriented teams to achieve significant results for everyone involved." "I create computer communications that grab the attention of teenagers and cause them to respond." "I save companies millions of dollars each year by unlocking the key to their employees' productivity." Such statements can stimulate follow-up questions or at least further interest: "Tell me more."

The reality is that few people know what they do best, and even fewer can articulate it to someone else. They've never really learned how to explain it so that others understand and see the relevance. Being able to do just that will set you apart.

Action Plan

As Peter Drucker has said, "Management is doing things right, leadership is doing the right things."[2] Have a plan.

In taking it to the streets, your main activity is communicating. And you will want to answer the questions: With whom should I communicate? And what's the best way to do that?

Some people are like bees, pollinating the networks of information and creating a buzz. They know people in the places where your gifts are needed. Write down their names and plan to call them. You can find them in associations, chamber of commerce posts, nonprofit leadership teams, and so on.

Second, work from the top down. Start by speaking with those whose word sways the actions of others. Go direct. Moses went to Pharaoh; Nehemiah went directly to King Ataxerxes; and Esther spoke directly to King Xerxes.

Those in top positions can direct you to others. They're not always going to bring you in themselves, but even if they don't act on your request, they influence others to do so. There really is a pecking order of influence. Imagine speaking to the human resources director and introducing yourself by saying, "I spoke to the president, and he encouraged me to speak with you about what I do" or saying, "The CEO invited me to share what I have to offer with you." That's much more compelling than an initial cold call to human resources.

Of course, most of us immediately think, *Who am I? Why would the top dog want to speak with me?* Remember, these are people just like you and I. They too are humans who have felt inadequate, gotten indigestion, put their foot in their mouth, and started out somewhere. Like you, they believed in what they were doing enough to risk it.

In order to take it to the streets, you'll need an action plan. Put it on paper. Create a targeted list of influencers you will speak directly to. List specific individuals you know or those in positions in organizations you want to approach: the president, the vice president of sales, the CEO, the human resources director. How will you work top down and knock on the doors that may be open to you even if the company hasn't posted a help wanted ad?

The Hidden Job Market

The hidden job market is filled with those opportunities not posted on job boards or in newspaper help wanted ads. Many job opportunities never show up as an ad or an official opening. A major newspaper ad can cost thousands of dollars. Posting an ad on the Internet can yield thousands of applicants who may not even fit the opportunity. So in many cases, companies just don't list the jobs.

As I (Tom) consider experiences when I was a hiring manager in the corporate world, some of my best hires came through the hidden job market. For example, I was racing to get a flight out of O'Hare Airport on a Monday morning. As I jumped in the airport shuttle, I looked up from my newspaper and noticed a sharply dressed man sitting across from me studying some notes. As I finished reading the sport section, I introduced myself and made some small talk. His name was Brent, and I learned that he was involved with sales and was on his way out of town to a meeting. I inquired more about his position and experience and found myself drawn to his positive mental outlook. He was upbeat, full of enthusiasm, professional, well groomed—the kind of person I would want on my team. He knew how to articulate what he did and had a plan for his career growth. "Have you ever thought about working for another company?" "Yes," he said. Though I hadn't been in an official hiring mode, I pulled out my business card, wrote the name of our local sales manager, and gave it to him. "You tell him that I told you to give him a call." Brent accepted a position with us and went on to become one of the top salespeople in the company. He found a hidden job market riding to the airport. (And I felt like I hit a home run for our company!) You just never know when you will have that kind of opportunity.

Many companies, hiring managers, and senior managers are on the lookout for talent. Some companies even give cash rewards to those who refer candidates. They want employees that don't need significant investment before providing value. Those kind of finds happen in shuttles on the way to airports, at social gatherings, at trade shows, and in training classes. They also happen when you proactively seek out the hidden job market.

Research companies, firms, or organizations that you could see working with. Read about them on their Web site or in reference material in the library. (See Chapter Ten to learn how to use the library and the Web in your search.) Read their mission statement and learn who's who in the chain of command. Dial direct to the hiring manager in each of these locations. You may find companies that fit your career calling. You may be able sift through numerous companies and identify twenty that are ideal. That's a good start!

Finally, as you take it to the streets, have your eyes wide open to the unexpected opportunities, the unplanned, and the serendipitous. Be open and aware of the people you run into and the opportunities that come to light. Equipped with a positive mental outlook, product knowledge, an action plan, and knowledge of the hidden job market, you may discover that the streets offer a wealth of opportunities with less competition.

Table 12.1 will help you identify your own targeted hot list of companies. Use it to keep yourself organized and focused. For each company you identify as a potential employer, gather information to help you access the correct person or persons in the organization. Table 12.2 is a chain-of-command chart to help you keep track of who is where at a given company.

TABLE 12.1 Targeted Hot List

Company Name	Location	Business Type	Commute Time	Interest Level

TABLE 12.2   Chain-of-Command Chart

Chain of Command for _____ **Created on** _____

Title	Name	Phone and Extension	Executive Assistant's Name
CEO			
President or chief operating officer			
Senior or executive vice president			
Vice president of sales			
Vice president of information technology			
Vice president of finance			
Vice president of marketing			
Vice president of operations			
Director			
Director			
Regional or line manager			
Regional or line manager			
Supervisor			
Supervisor			

CHAPTER 13

Step Up to the Plate

The Interview

IT'S THE BOTTOM of the ninth, and there are two outs. As you step up to the plate, you recognize it's do or die. You have the opportunity to bat in the game-winning run and lead your team to victory. If you pop up or strike out, the game is over. This is your moment. All eyes are on you.

Chapter Take-Aways

- Learn about the different types of interviews.
- Prepare for key questions to ask and be asked.
- Know how to follow up on your interviews.

Or you're asked to give a talk in front of a large live audience. The impact of this talk will influence and possibly change the course of key decisions. You've been asked to give the talk because of your expertise and experience. You have the knowledge and you've studied your material. But once you step out in front, all eyes are on you.

Anyone who has experienced such a clutch moment can identify with the stress or the adrenaline rush. We tend to identify players who lead their teams to victory with their performance; we expect them to keep winning. In the same way, public speakers know what it means to step out with no net to catch them: they feel their chest tighten and their pulse increase. Some let the pressure get to them. Others rise to the occasion and give their all. They pull it off and thrive in the limelight.

What happens to you when you're up at bat?

The interview is the up-at-bat experience in the competitive sport of finding a new job. So what's an interview? Obviously, we know it's a way to move along in a relationship to see if there's a fit between you and the company. It can also be

A time to share the strengths and credentials that your résumé identified

A chance to engage in dialogue that can move you ahead of other candidates

An occasion to get to know the company's culture

A way to expand the network of people who know you and know what you do best

A way to come one step closer to landing a job that fits your calling

This chapter will give you a window into the interview process and help you make the experience both enjoyable and effective.

Preparing for the Interview

Someone who has known Oprah Winfrey for many years commented that she has a remarkable ability to pose the most focused, relevant, and thought-provoking questions possible. He said, "If you put one thousand people in a room and asked them to come up with ten great questions for a guest, Oprah would have come up with those same ten questions on her own. Also, she has a remarkable ability to be fully authentic and herself in front of a live audience." Oprah is also known for her diligence in being fully prepared for her interviews. She does her homework.

These same attributes make for successful job interviews. You've prepared the most thought-provoking and focused answers and questions. You know who you'll be meeting and as much as possible about the company or industry. You've also done any needed inner work to relax, rest, and let go of performance anxiety. You've sat quietly to reflect or pray. You've visualized the moment. You've taken deep breaths and let your shoulders relax. Now you feel confident and fully trust your ability to be yourself.

Preparation Checklist

❑ I know my interviewer and his or her position in the company.

❑ I have a profile of the company and its mission.

❑ I role-played the interview with someone else.

❑ I know where I'm going and have done a dry run of the commute.

❑ I've prepared a written list of questions.

Following are some more tips on how to succeed in an interview.

Ask Good Questions

Don't underestimate the value of great questions. Interviewers expect questions from candidates, not only at the end but also during the interview. They frequently evaluate your questions and use them to judge your candidacy.

After all, if you are going to invest your valuable time and energy in something, shouldn't you know what you're getting yourself into?

Consider asking questions like these:

What are the two or three things you look for in every new employee?

What are the company's top initiatives for this year?

What led you to the company? What keeps you here now?

What can you tell me about the company culture? What's it like to work here?

What do you see as the company's top accomplishment in the last few years?

How does the company plan to grow?

Dress Appropriately

This is pretty much common sense—or is it?

Though I (Tom) am no authority on fashion, I no longer hesitate to coach candidates I work with in this area. A few years ago I sent some seemingly qualified candidates to an interviewer, only to learn later that their improper clothing may have cost them credibility and possibly even the job. One woman wore such a showy and low-cut dress that she raised eyebrows and caught the attention of numerous people in the company's somewhat conservative environment. Unfortunately, her choice of clothing led her interviewers to question her professionalism. In another situation a twenty-something man showed up to his interview wearing a suit so wrinkled that the interviewer later said, "looked like he'd slept in it." I guess that wasn't a good thing!

As the saying goes, you only get one chance to make a first impression. Don't underestimate the value of what you wear. The rule of thumb here is that it's always better to be overdressed than underdressed. If in doubt, dress conservatively and follow these suggestions:

Men

Wear what's culturally appropriate for the company where you are interviewing. (Remember, the interview isn't the time to demonstrate "I have to be me.")

If you're wearing a suit, better to be on the conservative side. Dark suits are usually best: black, gray, navy.

Polish your shoes and belt.

If you tend to sweat, wear a white shirt.

Groom your hair and nails.

Women

Wear what's culturally appropriate for the company where you are interviewing.

Wear dresses or suits of reasonable length and cut.

Wear shoes with low to medium heels.

Wear jewelry that is tasteful and appropriate for business.

Style your hair and nails tastefully and lean toward being conservative yet fashionable.

Handling Different Interview Styles

Interviewers employ a combination of different interview styles in their search for the right employee. Many of them will likely mix and match a number of different techniques to probe your character, elicit your response, or even shake your confidence. You may encounter one or more of the following.

Traditional Interview

The traditional interview focuses on helping an interviewer elicit what you accomplished in the past. Interviewers often use this method in prescreening or telephone interviews to learn more about the experience you presented in your résumé. Success here involves clearly articulating your past achievements in order to explain your credibility and credentials. Some of the questions you might come across include the following:

What were your results last year? Were they consistent with your forecast?

What was your greatest accomplishment in that position?

How many people did you manage, and how did they do?

Tell me about your retention rate in customer service. What was the impact of your new ideas for data entry on the department and company?

Behavior Interview

Another interview style becoming more prevalent today is the behavior interview. The person conducting a behavior interview has one main goal: to understand how your past behavior might predict your future performance and success. The interviewer seeks not only to discover what you've done but also how you did it in various situations. He or she also looks to see whether your chemistry and values fit their company's culture. Questions often test your reaction to an environment or your philosophy.

Practicing for this style of interview will help you feel adequately prepared. Have someone ask you questions like the following:

Tell me about a situation when you were forced to make a difficult decision. How did you go about making your decision?

Give me an example of a time when you worked with a team to accomplish more together than on your own. What role did you play?

What was a time of failure or difficulty in your career? How did you handle it?

Group Interview

The group interview offers a way to get buy-in or approval from an entire team during an important hiring process. Of course, the dynamics of group interviewing are compounded due to the individual interviewers' personalities and styles. Imagine sitting across a table from six people, each with their own expectations, styles, and personalities. How might you handle it when one person challenges you on every point and another says nothing? Which person do you focus on? The challenge here will be to manage the group dynamics as well as the individual questioners. Here are some suggestions for effective group interviewing:

Be sure to shake everyone's hand.

Make eye contact with each person when you begin.

Respond directly to the person who asked the question. You might even use that person's name: "Jack, that's an interesting question. Let me address that for you."

Distribute attention to everyone. Don't ignore even those who seem quiet or preoccupied. Sometimes the quiet people hold the highest rank!

After the interview write thank-you notes to everyone who was present.

Stress Interview

The stress interview is designed to put you under pressure and explore your reaction. Do you get rattled? Do you become angry or irrational? The interviewer's strategy is to pose demanding questions and relentlessly challenge your answers. Some of the questions may even seem oppositional or illogical. And, yes, this kind of interview can be stressful. But your job is to stay calm, to listen and focus on one question at a time. If you feel unsure about what they are asking for, ask them to repeat it. Here are the kinds of questions you may hear in a stress interview:

So why in the world did you do that?

You must have been mad to do that! Are you a crazy person?

Exactly why would you leave such a great job and take a step back in your career? That doesn't make sense.

One of the best ways to handle these kind of challenges is to follow up with clarifying questions. For example, they might say, "You really don't fit this position. What if I threw you in another role?" You might respond, "What makes you say that I don't fit this position?"

Warning: this type of interview may tell you something about the company culture, which may stress confrontation. On the other hand, it may simply be this interviewer's job to shake you up or see how you handle some of the day-to-day pressures you may experience.

Stages in the Interview Process

Now that we have broken down the preparation necessary and the different types of interview styles, let's address the interview itself.

You may go through three definable types of interviews in the interview process:

- The prescreening interview
- The phone interview
- The face-to-face interview

Prescreening Interview

The prescreening interview is a way to see whether you meet the minimum requirements for the job. Usually, it's short and to the point and is designed to quickly gather some brief information about your work experience. The interviewer is likely talking with a number of people and uses this process to sort out candidates. Congratulations, you're no longer just words on the page of a résumé. You're now a person with a voice.

In larger companies a human resources assistant, clerk, or sometimes even a hired recruiter conducts the prescreening interview. Although the interview may take place face-to-face, it's more often held by phone.

Phone Interview

A phone interview commonly takes place when the interviewee lives in a distant location. The interviewer may also use it to take a more formal or in-depth approach to prescreening.

Unscheduled phone interviews are not uncommon. Don't panic: someone at the company saw something in your résumé or background that caused them to want to call you. The good news is that you won't have much time to get nervous or over-prepare. The bad news is that it's difficult to build a relationship with the interviewer without eye contact and body language. Also, if you get flustered, the interviewer may hear the nervousness in your voice. The rule here is to relax, take a deep breath, and be yourself. If they've caught you off guard, you may even want to ask them to hold for just a second. Regain your composure, organize your thoughts, and get back on the line.

One other thing: smile. People can feel a smile through the phone.

The Face-to-Face Interview

The face-to-face interview usually requires a trip to their office or location. In larger organizations a hiring manager or someone in the human resources department typically conducts the interview. Once again the key is to be prepared, relaxed, and focused. Make sure you get adequate sleep the night before, and be alert and positive.

Be sure to give yourself plenty of margin and arrive a few minutes early. If something unexpected happens and you realize you may be late, call right away with a sincere apology and let them know that you're on your way; offer that you will understand if they prefer to reschedule. If so, set the date and time while you are still on the phone. But do all you can to be on time!

Body Language

Because so much communication is nonverbal, be aware of your body language. The way you walk into a room sends a message and communicates an attitude. When your words say one thing, your body should agree. Here are some things to consider:

Handshakes: match your grip to theirs.

Posture: sit comfortably forward without hunching.

Facial expressions: look them in the eye and show interest in whatever the interviewer is saying.

Note taking: making the effort to jot down notes keeps you organized and can also signal your professionalism and interest in the job. You might ask, "Would you mind if I take notes?"

Listening: give the interviewer time to fully ask the question before you respond. You might even restate what they've said: "So it sounds like what you're really looking for is someone possessing a strong sales aptitude."

Most importantly, you need to know cold the answers to these two questions:

- Why should we hire you?
- What do you uniquely bring to this position?

Follow Up

Send a handwritten thank-you note. A brief note of thanks is always in order. Sending the note may even demonstrate your level of interest in the position. Here are some thoughts on thank-you notes:

- Write legibly.
- Use high-quality stationery.
- Send the note out within twenty-four hours.
- Keep it brief and to the point.

You may want to summarize a key agreement point in your thank-you note.

Follow-up phone calls provide the interviewer with another chance to remember you and ask a further question. You might introduce such a call by saying something like, "Meg, I just wanted to follow up and thank you again for your time. I can see why you really like this company. I wanted you to know of my sincere interest and desire to move forward in the process."

Here are some thoughts on follow-up calls:

Prepare what you will say before dialing and have an alternate plan if you have to leave a message.

Have a key point you want to communicate.

Keep it brief. Respect their time.

Don't oversell yourself or your interest.

If the opportunity presents itself, ask for the job.

If you have to use voice mail, keep your message to fewer than thirty seconds.

Remember, the interview process is about building a relationship, listening, and communicating who you are and what you do best. It's also about finding ways that you might add value to the team or further the company's mission. As hiring managers have told us, it's very evident when someone is well prepared for an interview. Very often those who are prepared get the job over those who are not.

CHAPTER **14**

Closing the Deal

Y OU'VE BEEN STANDING outside the front door of the corner grocery store trying to sell raffle tickets for the last forty minutes. Fundraising isn't necessarily your
forte, but you understand the importance of raising money for your school team. Still,
sales aren't going well. Plenty of people have walked by and smiled but not much more

than that. A few asked what you were selling, but
in the end said, "Good luck" or "No, thanks" and
rushed into the store. You think to yourself, *Is this
just impossible? Will anyone want to buy these
dumb tickets? Maybe this really is a waste of time.
Can't the school pay for its own equipment?*

Does this sound familiar? Anyone who's ever
sold anything knows the inner battle with fear that
takes place in your head. *I shouldn't have said that,*
you think, *I should have said this.* The work of closing the deal takes risk and a determined willingness
to overcome the fear of that tiny little word—*no.*

This chapter will focus on one of the more
challenging aspects of the job search process: asking for the job and finalizing the deal.
This is not only important for the obvious reason of job and income, it's also about the
respect you will gain by standing up for what you need and what you are worth.

You're not the only one who's ever felt nervous about asking for the sale or
making the deal. In fact, the Bible repeatedly encourages the reader: ask and you will
receive. Without the asking, there is no receiving.

> ### *Chapter Take-Aways*
>
> • Get up the courage to do
>   what many fail to do:
>   ask for the job!
> • Learn how to close and
>   negotiate a deal that's a
>   win for both sides.
> • Finish strong and take
>   your network of relation-
>   ships and key contacts
>   with you.

The fear of asking might even be right up there with fear of spiders, elevators, and public speaking. For example, Ken, a forty-year-old ex-navy pilot had all the courage in the world when it came to flying jets but would readily admit that he feared asking for anything in business. After taking the time to look deep inside to discover what he was great at, he still felt somewhat stuck. "I knew I was designed to lead people," he said. "I'm good at team building and encouragement. But I still can't get the right job." After an intense few months of searching, he discovered a company and position that seemed like a fit. After three interviews Ken was scheduled for a final full day of meetings with the management team.

"It was obvious they really liked me," he said. But as the day wore on and lunch felt like a continuation of the interview process, Ken started to think, *Will they just string me along?* After excusing himself to go the washroom, Ken looked in the mirror: *it's time for me to just ask for it!* "God," he prayed. "I feel all the signs are pointing to this job and company. Give me strength to ask for it." When Ken returned to the table, he took a deep breath and confidently said, "Based on the time we have spent together and what you have seen from me, I like what I see. I'm ready to discuss what your offer would look like."

The table quieted. After what seemed like an eternity to Ken, the company president began to laugh. "We were wondering when you were going to ask, Ken!" he said. "Yes, we would like to offer you the job." As you might imagine, Ken felt an instant sense of relief. He asked and he received.

Here are some hints to help you ask for your own offer:

- Develop a confident attitude.
  Believe in yourself. If you don't, others won't either.
  If you really are the best person for the job, be able to concisely explain why this is the case. Write down those reasons in preparation.

- Look for buy-in signs.
  Start with body language. What are their eyes and their posture telling you? Are they leaning forward? Are they opening up their hands and arms? Are they smiling?
  Listen carefully for clues. Are they saying things like "When you start here, you'll . . ." or "We can't wait for you to meet the rest of the team"?

- Take the risk and ask!
  Be honest and direct. Tell them what you want.
  Set up a follow-up meeting or next step.
  Ask for a time frame.

Negotiate the Job Offer

A few years ago, Ron Shapiro and Mark Jankowski wrote a book called *The Power of Nice: How to Negotiate so Everyone Wins, Especially You.* After some humbling experiences in high-profile media negotiations, Shapiro came to the conclusion that "unlike what we see in the 'novelized,' 'Hollywoodized' moguls, from Daddy Warbucks to J. R. Ewing, negotiation is not war. It isn't about getting the other side to wave a flag and surrender. Don't think 'hurt,' think 'help.' Don't demand, listen. The best way to get most of what you want is to help the other side get some of what it wants. You want them to survive, even thrive, to make sure the deal lasts and leads to more deals."[1]

Some see the word *negotiation* as an invitation to disagreement. In fact, *negotiation* actually means the process of bringing two separate parties together. Those who negotiate pursue a common understanding. The outcome of good negotiation should be getting to a yes that doesn't create hardship for either side. Both parties should walk away satisfied and feeling at least some sense of victory.

So what are your nonnegotiables? What would you be willing to leave on the table? *Compromise* becomes a bad word only when you give away what you value deeply. That's why defining your core values and needs is so important. Be clear about your priorities. Know your boundaries. But when things creep below your flinch point, you may need to step back and look at the whole picture. As Steven Covey puts it, "Win-Win or no deal."[2] Both sides have to feel like winners.

Negotiating Tips

There's a saying in negotiations: "The one who brings up money first loses." Even if they ask you point-blank, "So how much do you need to make?," keep that information to yourself. Master negotiators know how to keep discussions focused on value and opportunity. They respond with questions: "Based on what I would offer your company, how do you establish compensation?"

Compensation will depend on the company, position, or location you're talking about. A player who hits a baseball only three out of ten times at bat can make millions. Meanwhile, someone who works dawn till dusk, never missing a day, may make only $30,000 a year, if that. It may not seem fair, but understanding the nature of compensation prior to negotiating can help you evaluate (put a value to) the position that you want. Some positions will create more impact or economic value than others. The impact of one job may create a ripple effect through earnings within and even outside of a company. Understand the impact that you will make if you get the job and work for this company.

Be prepared for negotiations that go the opposite direction than you thought. Case in point: Tom's father, a plant manager just outside of Chicago, once asked an applicant during an interview, "What do you expect to be paid for this job?" The candidate paused and cautiously replied, "I'm looking for $10 per hour." Tom's dad looked him straight in the eye and said, "I'm sorry. I don't have any $10-per-hour jobs." The applicant looked confused. "I only have $12-an-hour jobs." The man looked even more confused. Tom's dad said, "But I expect a $12-an-hour employee, not a $10-an-hour employee." As you might imagine, the candidate got the point. He was quick to say, "When do I start?"

You too should be prepared to be flexible during monetary negotiations. Look for ways to get your needs met while satisfying others' needs. Here are some other negotiating points to keep in mind:

Know your bottom-line need. What can't you live without?

Know the difference between what you must have and what would be nice to have.

Seek common ground. What do you both believe in and desire?

Do your homework on what the industry pays for the positions you interview for. Look on the Internet, check the library, or ask recruiters or career counselors.

When unsure, ask more questions. Never agree unless you fully understand.

If the salary is less than what you desire, ask for a six-month salary review.

Get offers and points of agreement in writing (for example, benefits, vacation, and bonuses).

Through the process of negotiation, be sure to clarify other aspects that will affect your ability to do the job:

- Start date
- Hours
- Dress code
- Training schedule
- Expectations of performance

After the Deal Is Closed

Now that you've negotiated your deal and have the job that fits your calling, you need to tie up some loose ends. Although this is a perfect time to celebrate, it's also a good time to finish well and prepare for your new role. You'll want to hit the ground running, so learning more about your responsibilities in the company will help you shorten the time to success.

Finish Well!

It may require some hard work, but be sure to leave a current employer on a positive note. Tie up the loose ends. Though it may not seem this way at the time, leaving an employer high and dry can come back to bite you. No matter how good it might feel to vindicate yourself or sing silently or out loud, "Take this job and . . . . ," don't burn bridges that don't need burning. Remember that the person you burn today may be your client tomorrow—or even your boss! With acquisitions, mergers, and employment changes happening all the time, you never know when you will meet these people again.

Take the opportunity to properly inform your supervisor of your decision, even if it's stressful. Don't let the word leak out that you're taking another job. Make sure you're the one to speak with your supervisor. Don't let him or her find out through the grapevine that you're leaving. If you're unsure, it's always proper to give a minimum of two weeks' notice—or more depending on your level of responsibility.

Say No to Counteroffers

After you've given notice, don't be surprised if your supervisor calls you in to her office and offers you a seat. "I realize why this other company is interested in you," she may say. "We feel the same way. As such, we would like to find a way to keep you. Would you be open to staying if we offered you a match or an increase to your current offer?"

You may think to yourself, *Wow! I didn't realize how much they really valued me.* But think carefully before saying anything. And when you do speak, you may say something like this: "I'm really flattered that you think so highly of me. But I've taken a great deal of time in thought and prayer, and I've not made this decision lightly. Thank you, but I am happy with my decision. I hope you understand. I do not want to leave with any hard feelings. I'm happy to stay and finish what needs to be done."

Be ready for the counteroffer. Unless you do have a message from God on this one, start with "No, thank you." Others who have said yes have fallen into the trap of staying in the same company—with the same problems—for just a little more money or a little nicer title. At the end of the day, they were no further along in their satisfaction or calling. They later realized the extra money didn't make up for their dissatisfaction or lack of job fit that had caused them to look elsewhere in the first place. Still others later learned that the counteroffer was only a deliberate attempt to keep them away from a competitor. This became all too clear when their new position was unexpectedly terminated.

Update Your Contact Information

Besides experience, past pay, or 401(k) rollovers, the most important assets you can take with you are your relationships or contacts. Don't underestimate these resources. Of course, you may have to honor noncompetition agreements, but your network is your own. You built trust and connectedness over time. Let those people know where you're going and what you'll be doing. Send them e-mails or announcements with your new contact information. Even more importantly, get their updated information (Worksheet 11.1 can help you keep track). You may even want to get their home contact information, because they too may change companies or positions.

Celebrate!

Now is your day of rest. You've worked hard to understand your calling, talents, and skills. You've searched, interviewed, and gotten the job. You've exhibited courage and resilience. It's time to celebrate! Plan a special dinner or getaway with friends or family for a few days. Decompress and relax before heading into the next chapter of your life.

Remember to thank those who've helped and supported you during this stage and update them on your new change and assignment. Enjoy. You've earned it.

THREE

Keeping the Job That Fits Your Calling

CHAPTER 15

It's Here—The First Day!

EACH TIME a U.S. president begins a four-year term, our country orchestrates an elaborate first day, the inauguration. Even before the election is decided, planners begin envisioning, mapping, and budgeting for the event. A small army of planners leaves nothing to chance. Military guards drill tirelessly, rehearsing each step again and again. Security teams undergo painstaking run-throughs. The president works with speech writers to pen an acceptance speech. Staff members study guest lists meticulously and carefully program receptions. From the president's wardrobe to the route of the motorcade, a bevy of people makes sure that the president's term begins properly.

> ## Chapter Take-Aways
> - Obtain practical wisdom to unlock the potential of a great first day in a new job.
> - Start a new position with not only the right information but a well-prepared body, mind, and soul.
> - Present yourself well; it can make a big difference.

Though it is highly unlikely your new position will begin with a military review or secret service escort, the same principle applies to you. Begin well. Your first day on the job matters. Although this may seem somewhat superficial, you get only one chance to make a first impression. And first impressions can last—especially if they're negative.

Most of us have at least one memorable horror story, a memory of a time when we just didn't prepare well. We made a hasty, klutzy, or poor first impression. We showed up to a formal event in sweatpants, spilled red wine on our date, or ran the wrong way in a football game. We still cringe when we think of it.

We're not advocating obsessive behavior, but we do encourage you to prepare well for your first day on the job.

Know What To Expect

Taking a minute to think prevents hours of trouble.

—Sign that hung in Tom's father's workshop

Imagine that you're about to spend a year living in a foreign country. You have only one week to prepare. What would you need to know to make your transition as smooth as possible? Would you get a book on the basics of the language? Might you learn the best way to travel, investigate the geography, or look into what kind of food people eat over there? You'd certainly have to plan where you will live and what you will pack. You might also want to find out as much as possible about the people—their customs, their manners, their values.

As you begin a new job, you enter an environment that's new and possibly even foreign to you. You've never worked here before. And while it may be similar to where you used to work, there are likely many differences. You'll be tempted to compare where you are with where you've been. Try not to do this, at least for a while. See this as a new adventure and a learning experience. The environment holds its own culture, history, and even language. Coworkers have their own social patterns and expectations—just as you do.

You may be tempted to go in with résumés blazing or expertise on your sleeve. That approach will rarely win you friends. Just the opposite may occur. What do we tend to think when a newcomer approaches us with a spirit of superiority? "Hi, I'm the best thing that ever happened around here!" Chances are that attitude won't foster good first-day feelings or inspire a spirit of teamwork. Humility is a virtue, especially on the first day. "Everyone should be quick to listen, slow to speak, and slow to become angry," says biblical wisdom (James 1:19). In more recent years, Stephen Covey has restated the concept this way: "Seek first to understand—then to be understood."[1] See yourself as a student. Do all the research you can in order to know what to expect.

Know the History

To really understand your new organization's present, you'll want to learn its past. Whether the company has a long and established history or is a recent start-up, history influences destiny. No matter what your position, you will now play a role in shaping, influencing, or furthering that history. So you'll need to figure out how things got to where they are right now.

How did things get started?

Who played a role in shaping the company's vision, culture, and strategy?

What were the successes and hurdles in the last few years?

What made the news, and what has the company marketed?

Who's filled your position before? If they've left, why did they leave?

Know What It Means to Succeed

Get off on the right foot immediately. On your first day, ask your direct supervisor, "What should I be looking to achieve over the next couple of weeks? I want to get up to speed as quickly as possible so that I can make a contribution. What could I do to be sure that happens?" Instead of convincing yourself that you really should know what to expect, ask, "So what is expected?" It's possible you won't hit that target, but at least you will now know the target. As the saying goes, "Shoot at nothing, and you'll hit it every time!"

Who's your boss? That may or may not be easy to define. Or you may have to ask yourself: *Whose vision, goals, or objectives am I seeking to satisfy?* Is it those of a board, a president, a manager? Who sets your performance goals? Serve them. If they succeed, you too will succeed. Your job is to keep the boss happy. As I (Tom) often advise people starting a new job, "Don't steal. Don't lie. Don't cheat. Everything else is legal!" OK, so don't take that too literally; there are probably some dangerous loopholes in there. But understand my point: do what it takes. You're getting paid to do what you do. They're investing in you because they believe in you. So learn what it takes to succeed.

Do a Drive Through

Murphy's Law of Commuting is that if anything can go wrong, it will, especially on the first day! Getting there will take longer than you expect—especially during rush hour. You will take some wrong turns, head to the wrong building, or wind up in the mercilessly slow local-stop elevator. You'll begin to experience high levels of stress.

And who wants to start the first day fifteen minutes late? Great for first impressions, right? Instead, you want to show up relaxed, awake, and at least fifteen minutes early.

So do a drive through. Map out your route, get in the car, and commute during rush hour. If you'll be taking the train, get the schedule and learn which train gets you there at the right time. Take the earlier train the first day.

Know What to Wear

When you do your drive through, look to see how people dress for work. There's no need to show up in a business suit if everyone else on your level wears jeans. On the other hand, you'd really hate to show up in jeans only to find that everyone else wears a business suit.

Whether we like it or not, the clothes we wear send signals. Whether you're a service executive, an office clerk, or a production manager, clothes will influence how others perceive you and how well you can do your job. Clothes don't need to become all consuming, but they will influence first impressions.

The principle is this: seek to fit in, without overshadowing others or drawing attention to your clothes. Think back to your interviews. What were people wearing? If you're not sure what others wear, be sure to get that information by asking the human resources staff or hiring manager: "By the way, what do people tend to wear at the office?"

Here are some key things to remember:

It's better to be overdressed than underdressed.

If you're unsure, bring a sport jacket or a blazer—you can always leave it in the car or hang it on the coat rack.

Men: have an extra shirt, an extra tie (in case you spill something at lunch), and different shoes with you. Women: have an extra blouse and nylons with you.

Men and Women, make sure that your shoes are well polished and if you are wearing a belt, make sure it matches.

Bring breath mints for dry-mouth moments.

Be Prepared

Prepare for your first day by taking care of your body.

Be in Shape

Your calling may not require abs of steel or the stamina to run a four-minute mile, but you'll want your body and mind to be in shape for this new phase. Though you may no longer yawn from the fatigue of a job that doesn't fit, you will if you're eating poorly, resting haphazardly, and exercising infrequently.

This may not be the time to dive into a new diet, but it's certainly a time to watch what you eat. You don't want to start your new job after days of gorging on high-fat, high-carb, and high-calorie foods.

Be Relaxed

Take the time to get away and relax between jobs. Clear your head, your soul, and your schedule before diving into something new. Get away to a nature preserve, the mountains, the beach, a field of flowers, or farmland. Be still and do things that recharge you. Go sailing, play tennis or golf.

If you've been through a time of stress in another job, career uncertainty, or just change, you will want to catch your breath. And of course, stay on your exercise regimen. Just be careful about starting a new routine that's going to leave your muscles aching or sore.

Be Well Rested

You prepare yourself for the next day by what you do the day before. Get the amount of rest you need to wake up refreshed. How many hours of sleep do you need in order to be at your best? That depends on you. Plan to do something relaxing before you go to bed: read, take a bath, drink something without caffeine.

Open the Doors

Once you're prepared, keep things in perspective. Relax and enjoy yourself. This is going to be fun.

Remember that the first impressions people get of you at a new company are more important than your first impressions of them. People are going to view you as if you were onstage. Even if you're not the day's central attraction, you're new.

Learn What's Going On

For the first leg of this journey, you must hunt and gather information. Gain knowledge and understanding from those who know best, from those who've been around for a while. Here are some tips:

Use a notebook and portfolio to write down people's names.

Be ready to call them by name the next time you see them.

Be sure to ask questions in order to understand your training schedule.

If you meet with human resources staff, learn how benefits work. Then sign up for the appropriate benefits.

Eat Lunch

If coworkers invite you to lunch, go. This provides a chance for relationships and acceptance to grow. If you're not invited, don't hesitate to ask, "What do most of you do for lunch?" The sooner you become an integral part of the team and start building community, the better. You may want to bring your own lunch just in case. I (Tom) even suggest bringing extra cookies to share. (Trust me, one cookie is worth a thousand words!)

Here are some other suggestions:

Order food that you can eat with just your fork, no spicy hot chicken wings to add to your tie or white blouse. You don't want to have to navigate or make a decision on whether to use your utensils or hands for food.

Don't order an alcoholic drink, even if they do. You want to stay sharp. You never know what you might say in slurred speech!

Be more interested in others than interesting to them. Asking questions about their accomplishments and history with the company will tell you what's important to them. If you're a manager, this will disarm your new employees, your peers, or your boss. Most people like to talk about themselves.

Answer questions about yourself: your background, residence, and so on.

Remember that others will respect you more if you avoid coming on as an expert. *Who in the world does he think he is? He just walked in!*

This Is the Beginning

Today is just a start. You don't need to get it all or make a splash. You don't need to volunteer for everything the first day or understand everything. In fact, you may want to enjoy the opportunity to be the student for a while. It won't last!

If you're a manager, make sure you don't start out as Mr. Nice Guy, then seek to be tough the next month. But don't go in as Mr. Tough Guy either. Asking more questions and looking directly into others' eyes will help them understand your approach.

Once the day is over, take time to reflect. Go over what you've learned with your supervisor and share what you've observed.

Finally, be grateful that you have a job and give thanks for this incredible adventure you've begun. It's time to head home.

CHAPTER 16

Foundations First
Your First Month

Y OUR FIRST FEW MONTHS in your new position provide the opportunity to lay a strong foundation, but remember that Rome wasn't built in a day. You're there to accomplish something, but this isn't the time to complete projects and achieve goals. It's probably not the time to knock down what you don't like and shake things up. Instead, this is your time to clarify objectives, set goals, and learn what it will take to succeed in the new environment. Consider this as your time to investigate. The first thirty days will provide you an insider's view into the world of your new position. It also offers your new coworkers a glimpse of you.

> ### *Chapter Take-Aways*
>
> - Know how to create support structures to establish your place in the organization.
> - See the things that bug you as potential opportunities to bring your unique view and experience to your new position.
> - Complete your own thirty-day review of what you've learned and need to learn in order to maximize your calling and gifts in this role.

If you've ever watched or participated in the construction of a large building or skyscraper, you know that the crew spends many months digging an enormous hole. At first, engineers pore over designs and study the makeup of the ground. Once the large equipment moves in, the moving, blasting, and digging begins. There's nothing aesthetically pleasing about it.

As you move into the foundation phase of your new job, the ground of your life and schedule will shift. Of course, there's the excitement of the new venture. But as the book of Proverbs (24:3 NIV) puts it, "By wisdom a home is built." Maybe you're going from a flexible schedule to waking at 6:00 A.M. and driving an hour to work. Or you may now be waking while it's still pitch black to catch a flight to another city. The key is to pace yourself. Laying a foundation is a whole lot of work, a whole lot of change, and its results don't feel or look that impressive. It's noise, dust, dirt, and a pile of rocks.

Just as a president's first one hundred days in office sets the tone of the administration and establishes the overall direction and policy, you will have a chance to get off on the right foot in your new job. Here are some things to consider in those early days.

Be Prepared for Some Stress

Along with getting married, having children, or buying a home, starting a new job is one of the most stressful parts of life. The simplest things such as logging on to your computer, finding files, or getting to meetings on time take up brain space. There are few no-brainers for a while. For example, if you changed positions, you may have been the go-to person. Now you may be in a position where you'll be seeking the answers. Now you're the person who can't find the paper clips or know who to call when your e-mail doesn't work. Don't forget: you are in transition.

Making it through this period of change can take time. And it will require knowledge, skill, and patience. This isn't a destination, it's a journey. So be patient and stay the course. Take a deep breath and relax. No one expects you to do it all in this time of transition.

Crawl Before You Walk, Walk Before You Run

Of course, if you're working with a company, the people who hired you understand that you're new. *I don't want to look foolish. I won't ask,* you may think to yourself. *I'll just try to do it myself.* You may feel like the new kid in school who doesn't know where the lunchroom is, not to mention which table to sit at. If you don't ask for help, you may extend the time it will take to feel included in your new environment.

Take this time to get organized and walk gently. All too often new managers or employees come in feeling full of fire and ready to prove their value and try to do too much. Why might we do this? Could it be we have a need or desire for validation that makes us feel we must do something relevant? Or do we just feel self-conscious and want others to like us? In either case, you may need to overcome a desire to prove yourself and call it what it is: insecurity.

Remember to crawl before you walk.

Create Support Structures

Creating a support structure through relationships will help you fit in with your new company. Get to know those you work with and build a group of supporters, people you can lean on.

This certainly involves more than just one meeting. If you've ever been in a musical, the director may have told you, "You need to always be in character, even if you're not speaking, because someone may be looking." The point here is everything that you do is in full view; things like body language can be as important as speaking because your staff, peers, or managers may be watching you.

Here are some points to ponder:

For Managers

Meet with your team as a group and individually.

Work with each person.

Have lunch with as many people as you can.

Listen before you react.

Ask questions: What can I do to help you? What areas do you think need fixing?

For Team Members

Have lunch with as many people as you can.

Ask questions first before jumping in.

Introduce yourself to everyone you meet, including the president.

Welcome input, but be discerning.

If you're not sure about something, talk to your manager.

Notice What Bugs You

At first you will see things that are impressive or interesting in your new position. You meet intelligent and hardworking people who've been doing what they do for a long time. You receive a barrage of information and intelligent-sounding policies.

But with a little time, a few observations, and some surprises, you may start to notice shortcomings. *Why do they do it this way? Why don't they do it that way?* Sometimes you see these overlooked issues yourself; at other times a veteran employee can start to point out the organization's underbelly. Once you start seeing and experiencing some of these issues, you may feel a bit of buyer's remorse. You may start to think, *How did I buy into this mess?*

Lynne was hired to be a chief operating officer for a fast-growing software company on the East Coast. At first she was thrilled by the opportunity and even saw it as a gift from God. But within three weeks, she started to wonder whether she should quit. Her honeymoon point soon ended when she came face-to-face with a corporate culture of disorganization and discord. "This place didn't have a clue about reporting structures or accountability," she complained. After seeing piles of unfiled reports and decisions being made willy-nilly, Lynne became irate and discouraged. "Things were being done twice or even three times. Meetings were missed or simply lacking any kind of agenda," she said. "I can't believe they're so inefficient! Why am I here?"

With some personal reflection and the counsel of an executive coach, Lynne had an "aha" moment. "Oh, so that's why they hired me? If they were totally organized, they wouldn't have hired a chief operating officer whose main gift was to create order and structure out of mess." The lesson: Lynne wasn't in the wrong place. Just the opposite: she was exactly what the company needed!

It's possible that in the first thirty days you may see things and start to wonder, *What were they thinking? Why isn't someone doing something about that?* And though it's probably not the time to make change, you may take note of what bugs you. Might this offer a clue or insight into what kind of changes you could bring in the future? Or even why you're there in the first place?

The Thirty-Day Self-Review

After you've been in your new position for thirty days, sit down and evaluate the situation, first on your own, then with your manager or your team.

For your own perspective, go back to the work you did in the first part of this book. Review your strengths, passions, and values. In what ways are you uniquely able to use those things? In what ways might your new position be challenging you to focus? You can record some observations and answers to these questions in a journal. You should also use the journal to keep track of your first month in your new job. Some people record events daily; others do this weekly. The point is to organize your thoughts, needs, and questions. We've also included a journal form for you to use in Worksheet 16.1.

Here are other questions to answer in that journal:

What have I learned in the first thirty days?

What are the things I'm most excited and encouraged by?

What people, projects, or possibilities am I most attracted to?

Where do I need to build bridges? Toward what? With whom?

Who are my allies and most vital teammates?

How can I become more organized? What tools or systems do I need to be more effective?

What additional learning will help me do my job better? How can I get it (classes or seminars, books, one-on-one interviews, on-the-job experiences)?

Now rate yourself: on a scale of one to ten (with one meaning "not a fit," five meaning "could be but not definitely," and ten meaning "I have no doubt that I'm called here and I fit"), how much do you see yourself as the right person for the job at this point?

Recalibrate with Your Coworkers

When you recalibrate an instrument, you realign the parts to get them working together. Chiropractors recalibrate the body's bones and muscles. Doctors offer ways to recalibrate our blood pressure, hormones, or medications. In the same way, in these

WORKSHEET 16.1

Journal Form: The First Thirty Days

Did I receive a training schedule? If not, how did I get trained? _____

_____

_____

Did my training schedule change? If so, why? _____

_____

_____

Do I completely understand my job? If not, what do I need to know? _____

_____

_____

Do I understand my benefits? If not, whom do I ask? _____

_____

_____

What possible problems do I see with my manager? _____

_____

_____

What employees do I have problems dealing with, and what is the situation? _____

_____

_____

Do I completely understand my role in the company? If not, what do I need to know? _____

_____

_____

Has someone reviewed my goals or performance requirements with me? What additional
questions do I have? _____

_____

_____

Does this position still fit my calling? If not, what changed? _____

_____

_____

What concerns do I have about the company or senior management? _____

_____

_____

What topics do I want to discuss with my manager? _____

_____

_____

first thirty days, look for ways to recalibrate with those you work with—and particularly your supervisors or subordinates. The sooner you catch slippage or misalignment, the easier realigning these relationships or restoring calibration will be.

The best way to recalibrate can be the simplest. Schedule a one-on-one meeting, a "how am I doing?" checkup. Whether you're an hourly employee, a vice president, or an office manager of a small organization, the principle is still the same: communicate. Ask them: "Is the work too much? Not enough? Are you receiving too much information? Not enough?" Ask for time to talk with your manager about what you see and what they see.

Your window for building a candid relationship starts right away. You can teach people how to treat you. So as you sit down with the other person, be honest in your feedback and ask what they really think.

Some managers ask for a written summary of your first thirty days. Others just want to know how your training is going and to see whether you're on track with your responsibilities. Use the journal you've kept to prepare for this meeting.

It's All About the Relationship

Finally, when all is said and done, the relationships matter most. Jesus's golden rule isn't just for friends, neighbors, and family. In your work, "treat others as you want to be treated" (Matthew 7:12 NAS). Of course, there will be people who won't like you and people you won't like. But most of us want to work in an environment where kinship, affinity, or a sense of mutual respect exists. Turning companies into communities isn't impossible. Most people tend to love workplaces that are free of backbiting and that encourage excellence.

People who leave jobs say: "I didn't feel listened to"; "They took me for all I was worth"; "They ripped me apart behind my back"; "Everyone was out for themselves."

People who stay in their jobs say: "They listened to me"; "I felt valued"; "They told me the truth"; "We were a team."

The key here is that relationship building in your workplace is about building bonds and connections with people around you, one relationship at a time.

Your first thirty days will go by quickly. But this is the time to lay the foundation. Take the time to reflect and change your course if need be. Build deep relationships. And remember, you are now working in the area of your career calling. You're in no rush. Your shift into higher gear is just beginning.

CHAPTER **17**

Staying on Track Long Term

YOU'RE HERE. Things are good. Going to work doesn't drain your energy the way it used to, and you're feeling progress and a sense that you fit. You enjoy thinking about your work, but it doesn't consume you. You sleep at night. You now realize you would like to keep this job or career path and not have it become a revolving door.

However, things may change. Like a sudden storm that comes out of nowhere, change is something you won't be able to control. And be assured, you'll be in for some level of conflict—no matter how great you are at what you do. You'll be challenged or forced to deal with it.

> ### Chapter Take-Aways
> - Be able to identify and be on guard against circumstances and people that can knock you off course.
> - Welcome and use conflict as a way to grow.
> - Have a checklist to stay the course in your job.

Getting here has taken you so long, how can you find a way to stay at it, to grow and even prosper?

We believe that most people quit too soon. Just when they're about to experience the greatest breakthroughs or the most significant progress, they abandon their position or don't fight to keep it. They tire of working, waiting, or fighting. The gold may be literally inches from their shovel when they throw down the shovel and resign. They may never know what could have been if they had endured.

If you've lived a while, you've had to take risks in work, faith, or relationships. Let's face it, you've known trouble. But we truly believe that getting to a place where things get hard doesn't necessarily mean that you're in the wrong place. Just the opposite: it may mean that you are exactly where you are needed. But if you're an agent of change or you encounter change, challenges, or possibly even chaos, you may be in a time where you need to stand strong. "Blessed is the man who perseveres" (James 1:12).

Expect Opposition

Study anyone whose calling and mission was highly effective or created impact, and you will notice seasons of heightened opposition and intense conflict, times when they questioned whether they should continue. The biographies of leaders like Moses and Martin Luther King Jr. and artists like Michelangelo and Rembrandt reveal times when they felt discouraged, overwhelmed, or underappreciated. A season of great growth and productivity in business is often followed by a plateau or even a decline. Bear markets follow on the heels of bull markets, sometimes with frightening speed.

How many truly good advances take place without some sort of a struggle? But in our experience and the experience of others we know, this struggle often expresses itself in discouragement. "Oh, this will never work!" "No one cares." "I can't do this!" If you thought you knew what you were called to do, you may even begin to question your call. "Maybe I'm kidding myself. It's not really my calling. I don't have these gifts."

Some of the most difficult attacks you encounter may be subtle or almost invisible. They come when we are not ready or just tired, overwhelmed, and running ragged. On the other hand, the in-your-face kind can be equally disturbing. Opposition can arise from where we least expect. Others lose faith, criticize, or just walk off. In the Psalms, King David, a man so clearly called to his life's work, wrote about this kind of opposition. David described the anguish of personal betrayal: "If an enemy were insulting me, I would endure it; if a foe were raising himself against me, I could hide from him. But it is you, a man like myself, my companion, my close friend, with whom I once enjoyed sweet fellowship" (55:12–14a).

If you've been called to leadership, management, or even entrepreneurial responsibility, you may have an opportunity to create positive and lasting change. You can make a big difference, but here's the catch: most people don't really want to change. Change can be tough. If you've been entrusted with getting people out of comfort zones or creating new ways of doing things, watch out! When you rattle a cage or call people to higher levels of action, they may just get angry at you. When things slow down or become harder than expected, it's human nature to seek a scapegoat.

Navigate Change

Though you may or may not be called to play the change agent, you will most certainly be forced to navigate some change in your career. Sometimes the track you're on starts changing, whether you're ready for it or not. Perhaps the personnel will change (people leave, are fired, get replaced); the technology will change; or your work environment may change because of mergers, downsizing, and acquisitions.

Some people think *change* is just a bad word. Have you ever met people whose fashion and tastes remained stuck in a bygone era? They wear collars, haircuts, or pants that were the in thing two decades ago. They're old-fashioned, outdated, not with it. It may be true that some of us find a decade we like, then just stick with it!

When it comes to your career, you're either growing and changing or you're dying. And many of those changes come at such a furious pace that it's hard to keep up. It's sad when employees get let go because they didn't learn the new computer technology, new systems, or new methods—but this is definitely avoidable. What makes the difference? Those who change and adapt survive; those who don't won't!

Peter Drucker, a well-respected and wise seer of marketplace trends, was adamant when he challenged workers to adjust, change, and grow with the times. In his book, *Management Challenges of the Twenty-First Century,* Drucker wrote, "More and more people in the workforce—and most knowledge workers—will have to manage themselves. They will have to place themselves where they can make the most contribution; they will have to learn to develop themselves. They will have to learn how to stay young and mentally alive during a fifty-year working life. They will have to learn how and when to change what they do, how they do it, and when they do it."[1]

Be ready and expect change, even embrace it. It will happen whether you control it or not. Think about it for a moment: What could keep you from navigating or making needed change in your career or position?

- ❑ Fear of what I don't know much about.
- ❑ Laziness or unwillingness to learn new things when I think the old stuff works just fine.

- ❏ Anger over those who keep forcing change on me.
- ❏ Too much stress in my life already. Change just makes more.
- ❏ I don't like what I can't understand or can't be an expert in.
- ❏ I don't handle stress well. Change creates stress.
- ❏ I don't like my supervisors, and I'm not willing to give them a chance.
- ❏ I have new responsibilities that are different from what I originally signed on for.

If you can figure out the obstacles to change, you can overcome them.

Navigate Conflict

Your tenure in any position depends directly on how you navigate conflict. And let's be up front here: you will experience conflict. People in any relationship with shared responsibilities, visions, goals, or dependence will see some things differently. That may seem obvious. But how often are you surprised by conflict or difference of opinion? It has a way of catching us off guard or threatening even the most meaningful projects. We can forget or lose track of the bigger picture when we lapse into nit-picking, protecting egos and ideas, or preserving our opinions.

We don't want to oversimplify here, but "blessed are the peacemakers" (Matthew 5:9 NIV) still holds in the marketplace. Those who find ways to work things out, to communicate, and to understand before being understood find a way to make things work.

When it comes down to it, many people who leave jobs do so because they couldn't get along with someone—often their boss, business partner, or coworkers. They may even leave smiling and ranting about the "awesome opportunity" they have elsewhere. But when they are really honest, their reason for leaving came down to unresolved conflict: "I couldn't stand working with Jerry. We just couldn't get on the same page about anything!"

You can probably name a person or two who doesn't seem to mind conflict. Some seem to even thrive on it. But most of us tend to avoid, ignore, or run from it. Perhaps we've paid the price for messy conflict in our past, whether at home or work. We know the pain or bear the scars of living in its noisy midst all too well.

As psychologist and author Scott Peck has described, this kind of avoidance or inability to navigate can leave most of our relationships shallow, creating what he terms "pseudo-community."[2] We end up walking on eggshells around each other, still saying a polite hello and asking about the other's weekend but not engaging. We're seething below the surface. Work starts to feel like unsafe territory, a drudgery. It feels tense and no fun.

In writing to a group of people experiencing conflict in the ancient city of Ephesus in Asia Minor, Paul wrote, "speak the truth in love" (Ephesians 4:15 NIV). In fact, this kind of truth telling was a hallmark of his description of spiritual maturity. When that kind of communication is lacking, we all know what happens: things start to disintegrate.

Speaking the truth may be as simple as using *I* as the subject of the sentence instead of *you*: "I felt misunderstood" as opposed to "You never listen to me!" Or "Judy, can we talk? I am feeling like I'm not understanding you." Language does matter here. Body language matters too. Be aware of your stance and the gestures you use as you speak; they have the potential to gently encourage or to berate and undermine.

Of course, your own resolve to speak truth and speak it gently, to love your neighbor at work isn't a surefire method to create a community of caring coworkers. Others get to choose too. As the Bible says, "as far as it depends on you, live at peace with all men" (Romans 12:18 NIV). And sometimes once you have done your part, the rest doesn't depend on you. You may need to extricate yourself from a caustic, unhealthy, or relationally damaged work situation. But "as long as it depends on you," seek to heal wounds. "Don't let the sun go down on your anger" (Ephesians 4:26 NIV).

So be willing to go to the other person face-to-face. Say what you're thinking. Listen to what they're trying to say. Care about your coworkers, your clients, and those in command. If you do so, your work relationships can be just that—relationships.

If you follow the items on this checklist, you will be able to manage change and conflict better. Think of this checklist as a note to yourself, a way to monitor and manage yourself.

Checklist for Staying on Track

❑ I keep a positive attitude at all times. I learn to encourage myself.

❑ I know and follow the work rules.

❑ I am flexible, not rigid.

- ❑ I volunteer for extra work.
- ❑ I take opportunities to learn new skills and continue my education.
- ❑ I network within my company and industry.
- ❑ I update my manager or board weekly.
- ❑ I know my manager's style.
- ❑ I understand the best time(s) to communicate with my supervisor.
- ❑ I understand my role within the company.
- ❑ I always ask for and welcome input.
- ❑ I listen and observe before giving input.
- ❑ I make myself indispensable by learning more than just my job.
- ❑ I trust that I'm where I am for a reason (even if it's not immediately clear).

CHAPTER 18

Recall

When Change Happens

T he phone rings inside the cluttered field office. "Hello," says the young corporal. "Yes, sir! Lieutenant, it's the general. He says it's urgent."

Quickly, the atmosphere changes to high alert. "What can I do for you, general? You want me to take on a new assignment?" For that instant, time freezes. "Of course, general. I'll do what it takes. Thank you, sir. Good-bye."

"What just happened, lieutenant?" asks the corporal.

"I'm not quite sure. All I know is that the general has changed my assignment. He wants me to head out right away. Seems like it must be pretty important for him to take the time to call me directly."

This kind of scenario is not all that unusual in the military. Called *redeployment,* it's a change of responsibility that may involve a transfer and usually leaves little room for choice. You're wanted, and you'll need to move out. Sometimes you know why; other times you haven't a clue.

The same sort of drastic change can happen in your career, though perhaps without the same urgency. Assignments end. Companies close. Corporations reorganize.

> ## *Chapter Take-Aways*
>
> - Learn how to navigate through a change of career calling.
> - Recognize the situations that signal when it's time to make a change.
> - Learn to discern between coincidence, need, environment, and the voice of God.

Sometimes these circumstances are within your control, or at least you see them coming. Other times things change instantly when the phone rings. You're asked to relocate or consider early retirement. Now it's time to move out or move on. We call this type of change a recall.

The way you navigate a recall may be more difficult than finding your calling the first time. Yet your response to a recall can unlock a whole new aspect of your calling. In fact, it may even be that your previous work was a training ground for what comes next.

Consider the ancient patriarch Abraham. When he's introduced in the book of Genesis, Abraham has had a long successful career as a sheepherder in a region called Ur of the Chaldeans. Though married to Sarah, the couple remains childless. Soon after resettling to the northern city of Haran, Abraham experiences one of history's most dramatic recalls: "The Lord had said to Abram, 'Leave your country, your people and your father's household and go to the land I will show you. I will make you into a great nation and I will bless you'" (Genesis 12:1–2).

What was Abraham's call? At age forty he might have said, "Sheepherder from Ur." He certainly couldn't have predicted what was coming: being a patriarch whose descendants throughout the world would claim a link to his lineage as people of faith for thousands of years.

Other notable examples of recall include the following:

A young shepherd who would one day kill a giant named Goliath and become a king

A Virginia farmer who would become the first president of a new nation

An African American woman from the South who would refuse to follow the cultural rules of that time and influence thousands to rise up and fight racial discrimination

These are all major, obvious, and public callings. But who is to say that a recall of a public figure to a role behind the scenes isn't ultimately more significant in the grander scheme of things? Was Jimmy Carter's most important accomplishment being president of the United States, or was it using a hammer in his retirement to build homes for those who couldn't afford them? Was U2 lead singer Bono at his apex when performing in packed stadiums or when lending his support for the cause of orphans in Africa? No matter your age or situation, your greatest achievement may still lie before you. What you or others perceive as failure or untimely change may be accomplishing a greater good.

Recall may result from one or more of four key changes:

- Spiritual change
- Passion change
- Season change
- Opportunity change

One or more of these changes can affect your next assignment.

When You Experience Spiritual Change

The result of authentic spiritual change affects the way we view our lives. Real spiritual growth transforms us from thinking *It's all about me* to *It's all about God and others.* It's a sense of clarified purpose and mission. When you experience spiritual growth in your life, it will affect the way you look at the world around you and what you do day to day.

For some this spiritual change is sudden and immediate. It's a whole new way of seeing life. For others the results may be the same but more gradual and less dramatic. It's an ongoing process with some signs of progress along the way. There comes a time when you realize that pleasure, power, and the pursuit of success aren't the be-all and end-all of life.

The key to spiritual change is the growth of a secure identity not tied to others' perception of worth or a pursuit of what will not last. As you grow spiritually, you find that your confidence springs from a center of peace. Your identity is secure.

Spiritual transformation may require you to act and make a change. Yes, you may need to leave your present situation because you feel torn and feel that doing your job requires you to compromise your beliefs and values. It may mean switching from for-profit to nonprofit or vice versa. It may mean leaving a lucrative practice or starting what will become a lucrative practice.

I (Jeff) left a position as the senior pastor of a church I had started in the Boston area in the 1990s because I could no longer do my job with spiritual integrity. Though

I fully believed in the mission of the church and loved the people and the nonprofit I founded, I realized I was no longer doing it out of goodness. I was spending more and more of my days trying to figure out how not to feel like a failure. I was hoping my good work would make me feel and be significant. I don't regret my involvement in it and love what has happened through this church and spin-off ministries. I do regret that I stayed too long, hoping that somehow I would prove myself.

Spiritual growth, by its very definition, will affect your life. You can't grow and do things the same way. And for you, spiritual change may mean

Not seeking the prestige of a position with a big title

Not needing a corner office in order to feel powerful or successful

Closing down a morally compromising business and taking a financial loss

Forsaking a lucrative job offer that will leave little time for family

Accepting a very public role that sometimes causes you to ask, "Who am I?"

Letting go of fear of failure and seeing your number one job as honoring God

Or spiritual change may mean letting go of your restlessness and being satisfied to stay where you are.

A new paradigm of work is beginning to take hold in our world today. More people are seeing the truth that when you do what you are, the universe (or the God of the universe) lends a hand. You were made for purposeful and creative work, not to be a cog in a wheel. It may mean that you can no longer keep doing what you've been doing. It's been for selfish gain, not for a higher calling. It's time to move into a purpose-driven field. Your awakened conscience won't allow you to keep investing each day in furthering the status quo. Change is inevitable.

If you're not currently there spiritually, you may still recognize that when you're connected to God, you just feel better. Isn't that what you really want anyway? Your soul will feel full when you return from a hard day of work, even if you're physically tired. You will create value without it feeling like a drain or an effort.

When Your Passion Changes

Just as you would in sustaining a significant relationship, you may need to invest to keep your passion burning and fueling your work. Conferences, reading, discussions, and most of all frontline involvement with your passion work best.

But passion evolves, changes, and sometimes wanes over a lifetime. And some people's painful or peak experiences may cause new or latent passions to emerge. The untimely death of Marge's sister from cancer ignited her passion to help others experiencing this hardship. She now works as an assistant in a cancer research facility and regularly participates in walks and cancer awareness days.

After his own healthy transformation by taking organic dietary supplements, Doug left a position with a technology company to foster a passion to help others find health, energy, and a better lifestyle. He now teaches on the subject and has created a market to work with others.

Of course, you will need to evaluate whether you're experiencing a short-term passion or whether this is really something to pay attention to. If you're unsure, turn back to Chapter Six to understand if it's a pastime or career. You might look at it the way you would dating. Is this newfound passion something that seems to sustain itself, is it something to do on the side? Or is a passion waning due to a change of season or other factors? Might this be a clue to consider moving on?

When the Season Changes

Sometimes change looms simply because seasons change. One part of life comes to an end, and it's time for the next. Children leave home, and parents find a new freedom of time and flexibility emerging. A season of caring for an elderly or ill person ends, and a season of moving on to new horizons begins. Financial resources become available, and it's time to make a move.

I (Tom) poignantly remember the day our youngest daughter, Leila, began college. As my wife and I drove away from that dorm room, we reflected on how our life would be forever different. Our son, Luke, whom we typically see once a week, doesn't need our daily input or involvement. Whereas our weeknights were once packed with baseball games, homework, and school programs, we can now decide whether to head out to a favorite restaurant or to catch a movie. No children's menu necessary! It's not that it's better or worse, it's just a different season of life.

You will encounter seasons in your life that invite a new introspection, perhaps a new calling. Winter, spring, summer, fall—is one season better than another? Only you will decide. And if you feel like you wasted the last season, or just coasted, might this new season present a way to shift into higher gear?

When Opportunity Changes

Opportunities are constantly presenting themselves to us. But when your eyes aren't open or you're distracted, you might step over an opportunity and never realize it was right at your feet.

For example, you've been commuting to the same office for years now in a job that you've loved or at least liked. One Monday morning the phone rings. On the line is an executive recruiter. She begins to describe a position you were previously unaware of. "Are you interested?" she asks. Or you're at a fundraiser for a major non-profit you care deeply about. Over a cup of coffee, the chairman approaches you and mentions, "We've been searching for someone with your background and the passion you possess. I realize you may not be looking to make a change, but the board felt we should at least speak with you. What are your thoughts?"

Or it may be as commonplace as looking through the newspaper on a Sunday afternoon. As you're thumbing through the business section, an ad jumps off the page. Immediately, you're drawn in and begin to daydream. *This is me!* you think to yourself. Is it coincidence? Or are you really supposed to consider making a shift?

You may face opportunities like these that cause you to wrestle or at least reevaluate. Is this merely a distraction, a selfish desire for more money or a change of scenery, or is something deeper going on? Is it time to pay attention? Although you're the only one who can know for sure, there are some actions or principles that can help you evaluate.

Does this coincide with or contradict what you already know about your calling, your passion, and your strengths?

Is this a recurring theme that continues to present itself?

Is this new opportunity about something bigger than you and possibly a divine knock on your door?

Is this a bigger venue that you are now prepared to step into?

If you had no fear, what would you do? Would this decision be easier?

What do your most trusted advisers say? If you are married, what does your spouse say? Your inner circle of trusted friends or family members?

If you were to create a chart with pros and cons about the change, which side would be more compelling?

You've navigated this kind of change before, and you've succeeded. This may just be the second part of your journey and the adventure you've been created for.

This chapter is filled with questions that only you can answer. But we do believe that nothing happens by coincidence and that much of life is a test. You are being asked to open your eyes to see where God is at work all around you. This is not to distract you from what is right in front of you but to enable you to use your greatest gifts and stretch your faith. You can't know the answers or all the what-ifs. But you can take the right next step forward in your calling by deciding if change is right for you or not.

CHAPTER 19

Caring for Your Soul

Staying Balanced and Sane

A S YOU BEGIN this chapter, we invite you to take a deep breath. Let your lungs fill and expand your diaphragm as well as your chest. Relax your shoulders and unclench your jaws. You have what it takes to live your calling and do your work for the long haul. Now it's time to find the balance, the rhythm, and the peace of mind to "walk and not grow weary . . . to run and not grow faint" (Isaiah 40:31 NIV). There is a balance and a pace that's right for you at this time in your life. Find it and avoid the extremes, because with the extremes come problems. Take a look at the following extremes and see which may apply to you:

Chapter Take-Aways

- Know how to discern the signs that your life is headed or is already out of balance.
- Apply the three principles of maintaining balance in life and work.
- Use tools to assess your current levels of balance and create actions that bring you back from the danger zone.

Good	*Not Good*
To love your work and look forward to it	To love your work so much that you neglect time with your family
To maintain an excellent work ethic and go the extra mile	To be unable to leave work and engage in rest, relationships, and recreation
To invest yourself in thinking about work issues	To be so consumed by work issues that you can't enjoy other parts of life

It's possible that if you are indeed working in the area of your gifts and passion, you may be tempted to run yourself into the ground, doing noble, great, or humanitarian things.

Each of us makes choices every day that influence or determine our life balance. Will I stay up and watch the local news tonight or head to bed? Will I stay at work an extra hour tonight or head home at the normal time?

Balance doesn't just happen. Finding your balance at work requires work! We're inviting you to be intentional and purposeful so that you can live your calling for the long haul.

The Scale of Balance

The balance scale (Figure 19.1) measures the equilibrium between work and the other valuable aspects of your life. If you were to weigh it out right now, what would your scale reveal?

Signs of Lack of Balance at Home	Signs of Lack of Balance at Work
Lazy	Thinking about work 24/7
Lethargic	Exhausted
Placid	Burning the candle at both ends
Disorganized	Working more than fifty hours per week
Half-hearted	Working evenings
Unmotivated	In crisis mode
Missing events	Having no fun
Feeling spiritual absence	Obsessed

Any or all of these factors can tip the scales, as will many others not listed here.

What Is Balance?

What does balance look and feel like? How do you know when you're in it or not in it?

FIGURE 19.1   The Scale of Balance

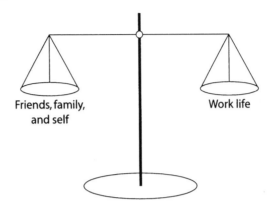

We know that work can sometimes require a great deal of energy and time. The responsible farmer needs to be up early and working late during the harvest season. The dedicated college student pulls an all-nighter to finish her term paper and study for the final. It's completely normal that at times you may be stretched, tired, or even depleted. You know there's a good kind of tired when you've put in a good day's work. Your muscles ache, or your head feels tapped. But like the tired athlete who's given their best on the field, you can't keep going without rejuvenation.

When lack of balance becomes the norm, that's a problem.

Senior Pastor Bill Hybels of Willow Creek Community Church in South Barrington, Illinois, described his own efforts to regain balance after a season of what he describes as "living in constant crisis mode." In his sermons he used the image of four gauges as checkpoints:

Physical gauge. How's my body doing? What do I need to do to operate with peak energy and strength?

Relational gauge. How are my most vital relationships doing? What do I need to do to express my love to them and prioritize our relationship?

Spiritual gauge. Where am I in my relationship with God? What do I need to do to restore this connectedness, as well as my life peace, perspective, and enjoyment?

Emotional gauge. How do I feel? Is my heart alive, and is my ability to feel empathy and excitement alert?

The Three Balance Principles

As you keep Pastor Hybels's gauges in mind, here are three principles you may want to follow to keep your life and work in balance.

Consistently Read Yourself

Reading yourself or looking at yourself requires you to be a student of what helps you operate at peak performance levels. The focus is on you, the person: your body, your energy, your overall health.

Of course, such balance means you must consistently "read" how much sleep you require in order to function at your best. Sleep rejuvenates, rebuilds, and enables you to ward off disease or sickness. Before going to bed, you may need to unwind from your concerns or your day's events. In doing so, establish a discipline of letting go physically and mentally. When you get in bed, take the time to breathe deeply as a sign and expression of faith, trust, and letting go. As you exhale and relax your body and your mind, release the tension and fear of not getting everything done. It's been said that "When you die, your inbox will still be full." You can't do it all. Let it go.

Though we sometimes see the physical body as less important than the spirit, the Bible actually elevates the value of the body, referring to it as "the temple of God" (1 Corinthians 6:19 NIV). Are you taking care of your temple? Are you feeding it in ways that maximize endurance and energy? Are you exercising as a way to release stress, develop strength, and increase stamina? Are you seeing rest as a necessary time, not just something to squeeze in when you're not busy with more important things?

Consistently Care for Your Soul

To care for your soul is to open the door for peace, purpose, and emotional rest to return.

The disruption of the soul takes place when you live under the constant pressure of unresolved anger, fear, or sadness. Physical rest, vacation time, or family time rarely suffices to renew a damaged soul.

The soul is renewed differently for different people. Some find that listening to music can be a form of caring for the soul. Others prefer time alone in the mountains or sitting by a quiet stream. Still others care for the soul by spending time with life-giving people. Active types may care for the soul through athletic activity. The key is to pay attention to your own soul. Monitor your internal temperature, and do whatever it takes to stay alive on the inside as well as the outside.

It's not possible to remove ourselves from all that would injure or stretch the soul. But if you want to bring the best you have to your work, your family, and friends, bring them a full and healthy soul.

Consistently Care for Those You Love

No one on their deathbed says, "Nuts, I should have spent more time at the office!" When most of us really step back and look at the bigger picture of life, we see our family pictures. We see our closest friends and those who count on us to be there for them. And one of the dangers of tipping the balance too far toward work is that you will neglect to care for your loved ones.

And yes, one significant way of caring for them is to provide financially. There's nothing wrong with providing a high standard of living and material possessions, but what those who love us most really want is *us*: time with us, quality time, time when work is the furthest thing from our minds and the person we're with is more important than anything. We put down our books, our papers, and our cell phones and look them in the eye. We do what they love even if we don't love it ourselves.

Balance means disengaging from work and being fully present in the relationship and in the moment: fishing together, doing yard work together, watching a movie together, serving together. It's about the *us* and not the *you*. Will you ever regret the time you invested with your six-year-old who couldn't wait to get a shake at McDonald's—just the two of you?

Some professions require a great deal of travel as part of the job, but you can still maintain the connection and balance with loved ones. Here are some tips to help maintain your relationships:

Call home every night—no exceptions.

If you're away for the whole week, pick up a postcard from where you're traveling for each of your kids and mail them on Monday with a quick note.

If you have a younger child, buy two copies of a bedtime book. Give the child one and read the other to him or her over the phone.

Talk to your kids about where you're going and where you've been.

Bring your spouse along on a trip periodically and find a way to stay over for a special weekend.

Worksheet 19.1 will help you assess your balance. Those who are way out of balance can use Worksheet 19.2 to get the scales back in balance.

The Balance Test

Instructions: Answer the following questions on a scale of 1 to 5 (1 = never; 5 = almost always).

Are you known as a workaholic? _____

Do you think a lot about work when you are with friends or family? _____

If you had only one year to live, would you make big changes in your work schedule? _____

Do you regularly work more than fifty hours a week? _____

Would family or trusted friends say you care more about making money than enjoying it? _____

Do you feel guilty about missing significant times with friends or family because of work responsibilities? _____

Do you sometimes jeopardize your health and well-being because of your work schedule or commitments? _____

Is it hard for you to say no to additional work opportunities or projects? _____

Do you feel overwhelmed at work due to high amounts of stress? _____

Do you spend more time at work than others you know? _____

If you asked your spouse or trusted friends to rate your balance (with 1 being a focus on self and family and 5 a focus on work), what would they say? _____

Total Score _____

Key

Less than 29   Congratulations, your life appears to be in balance.

30–39   You're approaching the danger zone. Go on to the questions in Worksheet 19.2.

40 or more   You're in the danger zone! Complete Worksheet 19.2 to get back in balance.

So here's the bottom line: Do what it takes to achieve balance. Here are some final tips to help you keep that balance.

Take time away. The drive to financial wealth or achievement can leave us richer monetarily but poor in quality of life and enjoyment of simple pleasures.

Recharge along the way. A car won't start without a battery, and the battery won't last unless it gets charged. You won't either. Stop everything else and do nothing but slowly recharge. Daily walks, breaks, or daydreams may be a way to stay recharged along the way.

Push back your boss and keep your family. Let your manager know that balance is important to you. It's really not the manager's responsibility to tell you when you need a break. Be honest and ask for the time you need.

WORSHEET 19.2

Action Plan if You're in the Danger Zone

What do you see as the root cause(s) for this swing out of balance? _____
_____
_____
_____

Prioritize the root cause(s).
1. _____
2. _____
3. _____

What can you delegate or let go of? _____
_____
_____

What actions or behaviors do you need to change? _____
_____
_____

Who might help you with these changes? Who can hold you accountable? _____
_____
_____
_____

CHAPTER 20

Giving Back

YOU HAVE SPENT these previous nineteen chapters doing some hard work. You've had to focus on digging deeply into your own heart and discovering your true interests. You examined your skills and moved toward your career sweet spot. If you've done this, you already live among a select group of people, the small minority who love what they do and do it less for the money than because they're gifted to do it!

And these are the two main things we want to leave you with.

People don't need to feel unfulfilled in their work! People today don't need to waste their lives doing things they were never called to do. We now know better, and we have the tools available to help. You can find happiness in what you do.

You can make a difference for someone else. If you've been fortunate enough to shift into higher gear yourself, you have the opportunity to give back. And you will have the energy and the motivation to do so. You can carry the message and the means to others. Once you've clarified your calling and your gifts, you can use these to benefit more than just you. What you do from this point forward has the potential to bring transformation that goes beyond the bottom line.

What we're talking about here doesn't mean that you won't have to sacrifice or that you won't really have to work. But this kind of giving back is giving out of a full

> ## Chapter Take-Aways
>
> - Know the whys and hows of giving back.
> - Discover practical ways you can make a difference.
> - Leave a legacy that will help someone else shift into higher gear.

heart and a full soul, not out of a sense of obligation, of doing what you "should" do. Yes, the receiver will receive, but in this new paradigm, so will the giver—often much more than they ever really give. As Saint Francis said centuries ago, "It is in giving that we receive."

The Greek word for *gift* (*charas*) springs from the same root as the word *grace*. To share your gifts with others brings grace to them as well as to you. It completes a circle of giving and receiving.

All of us know that it's difficult to get to our own heart and desires, let alone to others'. What part is altruism, and what is self-gratification? Just today I (Jeff) was talking with a business client who challenged my partner and me on whether our recommendations were based on his best interests or were, as he put it, "just another way for you and your company to make money." In some ways, I don't blame him, and I appreciated his candor. We need to ask ourselves: What do I give simply because it's what I do, and how much of it is about what I'll get? That's always worth examining and reflecting about. Is this all about me or all about others?

But we are appealing to your heart for a moment: Wouldn't you want those you care about to be as free as they can be in the forty or more hours a week they spend working as they are when they're off? We want that. And we believe you want that as well. Not for more money, not for the kudos, the thanks, or recognition but simply because we find life when we give life to others.

This book came to be in large part with the idea of giving back. I (Tom) own an executive recruiting and consulting company. Companies pay us to scout out talent, employees who stand out from the crowd. My way of giving back has been to teach classes and work one-on-one with those looking to find their way to a better career and calling. I'm amazed that almost every time I work with people, I receive much more than I ever give to anyone.

One day I received a call from Jeff, who had heard that I assist people in career transitions. We talked briefly and set a time to meet. As I listened to Jeff's story of helping people through facilitating retreats and coaching, I was intrigued by his passion for people and writing. Keep in mind that I was there to help him, but as I shared my story of helping others and writing this book, we began to see how we could support each other.

It became clear to us both that Jeff has a gift for writing and for unlocking people. I have a gift for discovering people's strengths and developing them. Together we created this book. You might not find as direct of a connection with another person as we experience, but you will never know unless you step out and risk.

Many people haven't heard the good news that there is another way—a higher gear. Many haven't had the opportunity to explore this avenue (perhaps due to a lack of funds, education, or encouragement). And many just haven't come into close contact with others who will spur them on to their higher gear.

Of course, we must all meet our primary needs before any other. Above career direction, we need food, clothing, and shelter. We need love and an authentic relationship with the Creator who made us. Those things are vital. But people everywhere also need to know that they don't need to waste their lives! Work is more than a paycheck, a benefits package, or early retirement. There is a greater purpose to all the work we do if we follow our calling. And that's the radical principle that underlies what the concept of a higher gear is all about. What people do on Monday matters just as much as what they do on Sunday. The message lost to many of us is that who we are and what we do is no accident. And work isn't something to just fall into but something that we choose according to a design and with intention.

In a world that can diagram DNA or split atoms, why wouldn't we be able to help a college student know what to do with their life? Why can't a corporation that can manage millions in assets help its people discover their unique niche, the work that will profit their lives as well as the company's bottom line?

In their book *Contented Cows Give Better Milk,* authors Bill Catlette and Richard Hadden share example after example of companies that are more profitable and successful because they reinvest and treat their employees right.[1] It does work, and it's no accident that these companies are known as great places to work.

Let us remind you of this ancient saying: "When the student is ready, the teacher will appear." And if you start listening, you will hear "students"—your friends, spouse, or coworkers—saying things like "I am so frustrated with my job" and "I feel stuck doing what I'm doing." Many of the people who say such things in their twenties are the same people who get to their forties and encounter midlife crisis, burnout, or depression—or just feel plain "blah."

What we're asking you to consider in this chapter is that you may be part of the solution, even if only for one person. That's right. What if you were to come alongside one person whom you believe in, help clarify their calling, and then unleash them toward fulfilling their purposeful work? Imagine the possibilities for meaningful work if they were to discover their higher gear. What kind of productivity and just plain happiness could be released?

Here are some practical ways you might give back:

First, live it yourself! You can't take anyone anywhere you haven't been willing to go. And when you do what you were created to do, and do it with diligence and joy, you serve the rest of us through your work. You stand out as a beacon of hope to others still stuck in low gear.

Share your story! Once you move into higher gear, your story and how you got there can offer a road map to others as well. With many stuck in a paradigm defining their success as titles, perks, and things, the wise words of one who's found a better way can change their lives. Especially for those who haven't yet realized that those things are fleeting and empty in and of themselves.

Mentor others. Whether it's through an official mentoring relationship or just over breakfast or lunch, you can provide what others hunger for: objective but caring guidance in things as important as career choice or next steps. You may think that you don't have anything to offer. Or maybe you think that others don't need (or won't want) your help. Even if you're just willing to listen to their struggle or their thinking, you may provide something more valuable than gold in their lives.

Tell them the truth. Sometimes what others need most is a dose of reality from someone willing to tell them how others see them. That message may be hard for them to hear: "You don't seem fulfilled doing what you're doing. Did you ever consider that this may not be the best use of your gifts?" Or it may be more encouraging: "I've noticed that when you manage a project, things get done. You seem to have some real leadership qualities. Have you ever considered moving toward a management position?"

Instill this philosophy in your workplace. Hold a core value that work starts with people. If you have management responsibility, encourage those you work with to know and clearly define their higher gear. Then take the risk to move them in that direction for their good—which will lead ultimately to the good of all. Life's too short to work around grumpy, unfulfilled, and misplaced workers!

Finally, pass this legacy on to the next generation. (Once again, it starts with you.) Actively observe and take note of the strengths and gifts in your children or grandchildren. Encourage them in those areas. Share with them your belief that they were designed purposefully and that you would like to help them succeed in discovering and living their calling.

You need to know that nothing happens without a purpose. If you've spent many years living without this knowledge or without the opportunity to live it out, it's not too late. And your pain may be what helps another find understanding and hope.

Someday it will all become clear. In the meantime our job is to act on the light we have and help others do the same.

May you be blessed beyond measure as you live to the fullest and help others do the same.

Don't look back! It's time for you to shift yourself into higher gear.

Appendix: One Hundred Things to Remember

1. Manage your time by planning out your week ahead of time.

2. Set daily, weekly, and monthly goals.

3. Spend 60 percent of your time networking.

4. Keep track of the résumés you've sent out.

5. If you need to work while searching for a new job, try to work at night and search during the day.

6. Attitude is everything. During a phone interview people can "hear" the expression on your face, so use a mirror during the interview.

7. Know your long- and short-term goals before the interview.

8. Know what you want (money, title, location, job, etc.) before you interview.

9. Put together a brag book of awards, letters, and references.

10. Know what your references will say, even about your weaknesses.

11. Handshakes count. Firmness shows confidence. The key is to match the other person's grip.

12. Eye contact during interviews can make you or break you. What do your eyes say?

13. Drive to your interview before the interview day so that you know the way.

14. Have questions ready before the interview.

15. Get a business card with an e-mail address or mailing address to enclose with your thank-you note.

16. Always send thank-you notes for either informational or job interviews.

17. After you land your job, update your résumé.

18. Have answers to these questions: How much money do I need? How much do I want?

19. Have three people proofread your résumé before you send it out.

20. Network today.

21. Take the time to open yourself and think about direction and calling.

22. Do a practice interview with someone who will be honest and direct.

23. Prepare and practice a ten-second pitch about what you are looking for and what you've done.

24. Call former employees to network about possible jobs.

25. Call your former bosses.

26. Develop a network list and build it for a lifetime.

27. Create your own Web site with your résumé on AOL, Yahoo, or another Internet service provider.

28. Ask God for direction—then listen.

29. Create more than one résumé if needed, Chronological vs. Functional and one personalized to the company and position.

30. During an interview over a meal, order something that you'll be able to eat with a fork.

31. Never order finger food or a sandwich during a lunch or dinner interview.

32. Review the company's mission statement before you interview.

33. List your key words at the bottom of your résumé and highlight them in white so that software programs will pick it up.

34. Listen to the interviewer's questions. If you don't understand, ask them to repeat them.

35. Never bad-mouth your former company or boss.

36. Take a risk today: call someone you don't know.

37. Always be early for an interview.

38. Don't ask about money first thing.

39. Know where your talents lie. Be realistic.

40. Ask five friends what they could see you doing well.

41. Spend a day at the library doing job research.

42. Take an afternoon and dream about what your dream job is.

43. Tell others exactly what your dream job is and have them watch for it.

44. Review every interview in writing and then review your notes before your next interview.

45. If the job's not right for you, think about whom it might fit. That person could help you out in the long run.

46. Listen for the clues to what your career calling is.

47. List your five greatest strengths.

48. Know the difference in interview styles.

49. Complete an assessment of yourself such as the Myers–Briggs test. Most are available online or at your local college or career center.

50. Know what your values are and stick to them even if it means passing up an immediate opportunity. Take a stand for long-term placement.

51. Look at the *Occupational Outlook Handbook.*

52. You can't fall off the floor; take a risk.

53. Be prepared to interview in an elevator or anywhere.

54. Look for people to introduce yourself to in unexpected places: in a coffee shop, in a limo or bus, on an airplane.

55. Don't burn bridges with employers, employees, or recruiters.

56. Pray, ask, listen, react.

57. Consider using a recruiter, but if you do, stay on top of him or her.

58. Call old classmates from college or high school.

59. What do you dream about doing?

60. Don't let someone tell you that you can't.

61. Be realistic about your skills, strengths, and talents.

62. Build relationships first, then job leads.

63. Be patient and stay the course.

64. Do not come into a new job like a roaring bull.

65. Introduce yourself to everyone.

66. Create an action room or a place to work on finding your career calling and your job.

67. Make an appointment with a reference librarian.

68. Know the skills that you have.

69. Match your mission to your company's mission.

70. Get to know your peers by asking them to lunch.

71. Be well rested and take time to relax before starting a new job.

72. Keep a journal.

73. Lose the battle, win the war.

74. Know your manager's or supervisor's management style.

75. Know your role. If you need to, ask for a job description.

76. Use the Golden Rule when dealing with people.

77. Be prepared and expect change.

78. If you don't have allies at work, find them.

79. Review the clues from your past to teach yourself about your strengths and gifts.

80. Look for the signs and clues that your calling may be changing.

81. There really is a hidden job market out there. Go and find it.

82. Take time to celebrate.

83. Get off to a good start your first day: be prepared.

84. Deal with conflict. Expect it and use it to grow.

85. Look for ways to create a win-win situation on both sides.

86. Don't gossip at work. You never know who is listening.

87. Listen, observe, ask, and then respond.

88. Create a balance between your work and life.

89. Take time to recharge.

90. Look for ways to help others on their path to calling.

91. Pray.

92. Work through the exercises in this book to find your calling.

93. Have a plan and work it.

94. Know that there are going to be course corrections to your calling. Welcome them.

95. You may be in a difficult situation for a reason. God may need you there.

96. Remember: it's a journey, not a destination.

97. When you're not sure, ask.

98. Being great at work takes work.

99. Be prepared for the future. It will find you.

100. Help unlock someone today.

Notes

Introduction

1. Michelangelo quotes (Italian Sculptor, painter, architect, and poet, considered the creator of the Renaissance, 1475–1564. Retrieved February, 2005, from http://en.thinkexist.com/quotation.

Chapter One

1. Quoted in Stephen Covey, *The 7 Habits of Highly Effective People* (New York: Simon & Schuster, 1989) p. 33.
2. Quoted in P. Palmer, *Let Your Life Speak* (San Francisco: Jossey-Bass, 2000) p. 11.
3. Mattson and Miller, *Finding a Job You Can Love* (Nashville, Tenn: Thomas Nelson, 1982) p. 60R.
4. F. Buechner, *Wishful Thinking: A Seeker's ABC* (San Francisco: Harper, 1993) p. 119.
5. *Mr. Holland's Opus*, directed by Stephen Herek (1995; Hollywood Ca: Hollywood Pictures).

Chapter Two

1. *Forrest Gump*, directed by Robert Zemeckis (1995; Hollywood, Ca: Parmount Pictures).
2. R. Warren, *The Purpose Driven Life* (Grand Rapids, Mich: Zondervan, 2002) p. 17.
3. S. Kierkegaard, *Prayers of Kierkegaard* (University of Chicago Press, 1956) p. 156.
4. Winston Churchill, speech to Harrow School, England, Oct 29, 1941; speech to Westminster College, Fulton, Miss., March 5, 1946.
5. Quoted in P. Palmer, *Let Your Life Speak* (San Francisco: Jossey-Bass, 2000) p. 11.

Chapter Three

1. B. Buford, *Halftime* (Grand Rapids, Mich: Zondervan, 1994) p. 81.
2. S. Lake, Ed.D., "Life Compass, How to Fulfill Your Purpose." Unpublished manscript, p. 49.

Chapter Four

1. H. Smith, *Ten Natural Laws of Successful Time and Life Management* (New York: Time Warner, 1994) p. 3.

Chapter Six

1. John Ortberg, *If You Want to Walk on Water You've Got to Get Out of the Boat* (Grand Rapids, Mich: Zondervan, 2001) cover title.

Chapter Seven

1. *It's a Wonderful Life*, directed by Frank Capra (1947; Hollywood Ca: Liberty Films).

Chapter Eight

1. *The Return of the Pink Panther*, directed by Blake Edwards (1975; Hollywood, Ca: United Artists City).

Chapter Eleven

1. H. Mackay, *Dig Your Well Before You're Thirsty* (New York: Doubleday, 1990) p. 11.

Chapter Twelve

1. *Wall Street*, directed by Oliver Stone (1987, Hollywood, Ca: 20th Century Fox).
2. Quoted in Stephen Covey, *The 7 Habits of Highly Effective People* (New York: Simon & Schuster, 1989) p. 101.

Chapter Fourteen

1. R. Shapiro and M. Jankowski, *The Power of Nice: How to Negotiate so Everyone Wins, Especially You* (New York: Wiley, 1998), p. 8.
2. Stephen Covey, *The 7 Habits of Highly Effective People* (New York: Simon & Schuster, 1989) p. 213.

Chapter Fifteen

1. Stephen Covey, *The 7 Habits of Highly Effective People* (New York: Simon & Schuster, 1989) p. 237.

Chapter Seventeen

1. P. Drucker, *Management Challenges of the Twenty-First Century* (New York: HarperCollins 1999) p. 163.

2. S. Peck, *The Different Drum* (New York, NY: Simon and Schuster, 1987) p. 87.

Chapter Twenty

1. B. Catlette and R. Hadden, *Contented Cows Give Better Milk* (Germantown, Tenn: Saltillo Press, 1998).

About the Authors

TOM SICILIANO is president and founder of Integrity Recruiting & Consulting Inc., a national recruitment and consulting firm. His company specializes in working with companies to strengthen the quality of their sales and management teams.

Prior to starting Integrity Recruiting & Consulting Inc., Tom served in senior sales leadership positions at two highly respected Fortune 500 companies, Aramark and Corporate Express, winning numerous prestigious awards for his leadership and results. He is also a principal with the Cimmaron Group, a consulting company focused on leadership development. Tom is a strategist who has been recognized for his ability to develop people, build teams, and help companies achieve their goals.

Tom speaks regularly to organizations across the country. This includes addressing corporate conventions on recruiting and retention, as well as helping corporations with their vision and sales results. He also speaks to career centers, helping thousands of people with his interactive lectures.

Tom is a Columbus University graduate with a degree in business administration.

Tom, his wife, Suzi, and their children, Luke and Leila, live near Chicago.

JEFF CALIGUIRE, a financial consultant with Smith Barney in Chicago, works with individuals, businesses, and nonprofit organizations seeking to purposefully unite their passion, mission, and vision with a comprehensive financial strategy. Along with his private wealth-management team, Jeff helps families and foundations create a blueprint for their future funding that begins with clearly defining and understanding their unique calling and goals—the higher gear.

For more than a decade, Jeff worked in the nonprofit world. He founded Operation Beacon Street Inc. and served as its president, as well as serving as senior pastor of Beacon Community Church in the Boston area. Jeff also cofounded the Boston Sports Fellowship and cohosted Leadership Refineries team for business leaders with author Ralph Mattson. Jeff's other books include *Leadership Secrets of Saint Paul* (Honor Books, 2003) and *Write for Your Soul: The Whys and Hows of Journaling* (Soul Care Communications, 2000), which he cowrote with his wife, Mindy. Jeff facilitates forums and speaks to entrepreneurs and others wanting to get into higher gear in their career, their finances, or their overall life purpose.

Jeff is a graduate of Cornell University with a major in government and also holds a master's of theology degree from Dallas Theological Seminary. He and Mindy have three sons, Jeffrey, Jonathan, and Joshua (the J-Team).

Other Books of Interest

The Anger Trap:
Free Yourself from the Frustrations
That Sabotage Your Life
Les Carter, Ph.D.

ISBN: 0–7879–6880–3   Paper
www.josseybass.com

"*The Anger Trap* is a masterfully written book, offering penetrating insights into the factors that can imprison individuals in unwanted patterns of frustration. With his well-developed insights and using case examples, Les Carter carefully explains how you can change your thinking, your communication, and your behavior as you release yourself from the ravages of anger gone bad."

—from the Foreword by Frank Minirth, M.D.

"Les Carter has assimilated his years of experience counseling people trapped by anger into a book that I believe will prove helpful to many readers. *The Anger Trap* offers fresh information and understanding that can lead to recovery and reconciliation."

—Zig Ziglar, author and motivational speaker

"The best book on anger out there. Five stars!"
—Dr. Tim Clinton, president, American Association of Christian Counselors

Dr. Les Carter—a nationally recognized expert on the topics of conflict resolution, emotions, and spirituality, and coauthor of the bestselling *The Anger Workbook*—has written this practical book that strips away common myths and misconceptions to show viable ways to overcome unhealthy anger and improve relationships. With gentle spiritual wisdom and solid psychological research, Dr. Carter guides you to creating a better, happier life for yourself, your family, and your coworkers.

Les Carter, Ph.D., maintains his practice at the Southlake Psychiatry and Counseling Clinic in Southlake, Texas. Previously, Dr. Carter was with the Minirth Clinic for twenty-five years. He is a nationally recognized expert on topics including conflict resolution, emotions and spirituality, and marriage and family relationships. He is the author or coauthor of twenty books including the bestselling *The Anger Workbook, The Anger Trap, The Anger Workbook for Christian Parents,* and *The Freedom From Depression Workbook*. Dr. Carter can be reached at www.drlescarter.com.

Other Books of Interest

Grace and Divorce
God's Healing Gift for Those Whose Marriages Fall Short
Les Carter, Ph.D.

ISBN : 0–7879–7581–8   Hardcover

www.josseybass.com

"At last! *Grace and Divorce* achieves harmonious balance of biblical doctrine and biblical grace toward divorce. This is a very practical, user-friendly book that pastors, counselors, and church leaders will turn to again and again as they minister to hurting people."

—Steve Grissom, Founder, DivorceCare

". . . This book is long overdue. It will be an invaluable purchase, and a gift of grace, for those experiencing both the pain of divorce and the disapproval of fellow believers."

—Freda V. Crews, D.Min., Ph.D., host of the internationally syndicated television program *Time for Hope*

Divorce rates for evangelical Christians are just as high as for any other segment of American society, but the experience is made even more painful by the judgmental attitudes divorcees encounter in their churches and from their clergy. By offering a deeper and more nuanced scriptural explanation of the role of grace (and humanity's need for it) in our understanding of divorce, *Grace and Divorce* seeks to uphold the ideals of marriage while emphasizing how love and acceptance can still be given to those whose marriages have not attained the ideal.

Les Carter, Ph.D., maintains his practice at the Southlake Psychiatry and Counseling Clinic in Southlake, Texas. Previously, Dr. Carter was with the Minirth Clinic for twenty-five years. He is a nationally recognized expert on topics including conflict resolution, emotions and spirituality, and marriage and family relationships. He is the author or coauthor of twenty books including the bestselling *The Anger Workbook, The Anger Trap, The Anger Workbook for Christian Parents,* and *The Freedom From Depression Workbook*. Dr. Carter can be reached at www.drlescarter.com.

Other Books of Interest

Christian Reflections on The Leadership Challenge
James M. Kouzes & Barry Z. Posner, Editors

ISBN : 0-7879-6785-8   Hardcover

www.josseybass.com

"... *Christian Reflections on The Leadership Challenge* is a book for everyone who aspires to be the best leader they can be by investing their lives in others."

—From the Foreword by John C. Maxwell, Founder, The INJOY Group

"... facilitates a positive guidance role."

—*Publishers Weekly*

Christian Reflections on The Leadership Challenge gathers together in one place a remarkable collection of leaders who share insights on faith and leadership. Well-grounded in research, this reflective and practical book shows how Christian leaders–no matter the setting–put into place The Five Practices of Exemplary Leadership®–Model the Way, Inspire a Shared Vision, Challenge the Process, Enable Others to Act, and Encourage the Heart.

Jim Kouzes and Barry Posner are the award-winning coauthors of several best-selling books, including *The Leadership Challenge, Credibility,* and *Encouraging the Heart.* Jim is also an executive fellow at the Center for Innovation and Entrepreneurship at the Leavey School of Business, Santa Clara University, and chairman emeritus of the Tom Peters Company. Barry is the dean of the Leavey School of Business and professor of leadership at Santa Clara University.